PRINCES OF THE CHURCH

PRINCES OF THE CHURCH

BY

W. ROBERTSON NICOLL

SECOND EDITION

Wipf and Stock Publishers
199 W 8th Ave, Suite 3
Eugene, OR 97401

Princes of the Church
By Nicoll, W. Robertson
ISBN 13: 978-1-55635-158-7
ISBN 10: 1-55635-158-5
Publication date 12/22/2006
Previously published by Hodder and Stoughton, 1923

PREFATORY NOTE

SINCE the *British Weekly* was founded in 1886 I have been in the habit of writing tributes to notable figures in the Christian world. Out of a large number the present book has been made up. The selection is due to my friend and colleague, Miss Jane T. Stoddart, who has also helped me generously in the revision of the proofs.

Practically no change has been made in the papers, but the date of publication in each instance has been put at the end of the article, and this will explain contemporary allusions.

BAY TREE LODGE,
HAMPSTEAD,
September 1921.

CONTENTS

PROFESSOR ELMSLIE

PREVIOUS announcements will have in some degree prepared our readers for the heavy tidings of Professor Elmslie's death. For some months he had not been well. He found it necessary to take longer holidays than usual during the summer, and, in accordance with medical advice, spent most of September in the Engadine. Soon after his return he complained of illness: one day he fainted in a railway station, and he consented to reduce his public work, and to undertake not more than one sermon on a Sunday. He had engaged to preach anniversary sermons on Sunday, November 3, for his friend the Rev. John Watson, of Sefton Park, Liverpool, who had himself been seriously ill. But he complained of neuralgia, and when the time came his wife thought it desirable to accompany him. In the forenoon he preached with great vigour, but by medical advice remained at home in the evening. He came back to London still far from well. On Thursday he was compelled to lie down. His temperature was very high, and he suffered from distressing pains in the head. All attempts to reduce the temperature failed, and on Tuesday the doctors declared the disease to be typhoid with complications. Delirium followed, with intervals of collapse. There was very little hope from the first, and the fever raged on till the early morning of Saturday, when he quietly breathed his last.

Scarcely any death could have made a greater rent, not only in his own circle, but in very many outside of it. He was more than an object of admiration and hope to multitudes: by all who knew him and thousands who did not, he was regarded with deep affection. His chief ambition was to be a comforter in this sorrowful world, and he succeeded. It is fit, therefore, that something of his noble and loving life should be set down by one who had the privilege of close intercourse, though in the presence of such a loss we hardly know how to write either of it or him.

The external events of his life are soon told. He was a son of the manse, his father, the Rev. William Elmslie, who survives him, being minister of the Free Church, Insch, Aberdeenshire, where he was born in 1848. Some well-known men are natives of the same somewhat remote region. Not many miles off is the Free Church manse which was the birthplace of Professor Robertson Smith. George Macdonald, the poet, is a native of Huntly, a small town in the same neighbourhood. From the first Elmslie was noted for his winning manner, his lovable character, his high conscientiousness, and his unsparing industry. He went to the University of Aberdeen, where he proved himself a most brilliant student, taking his degree of M.A. at a very early age, with the gold medal awarded to the best scholar of the year. In a short time he acted as Assistant Professor of Natural Philosophy. In after life his face changed little: he retained his youthful appearance, especially at a distance, though nearer at hand in the last year one noted too often traces of weariness and suffering. His gift of silver speech was very early shown: we remember him addressing an assembly of students when he cannot have been more than eighteen, with the same ease and charm which so many came afterwards to admire. Among the students he was a peculiar favourite: success never spoiled him. Although tempted to go to Cambridge, he had made up his mind to be a Presbyterian minister, and went to the New College, Edinburgh, for his theological training. There he studied Hebrew under Professor A. B. Davidson, of whom he has written so eloquently in the *Expositor*. Here, too, he was in every way a distinguished student, and the highest hopes were cherished of his career as a preacher. Many important positions in the Free Church were open to him, but he did not wish to settle down too soon, and accepted an offer to go to Regent Square Church, London, to act as assistant to Dr. Oswald Dykes. In this way it turned out that his ministerial life was spent not in Scotland, but in the Presbyterian Church of England.

His stay at Regent Square was a very happy period in his life. For Dr. Dykes, both as a preacher and as a friend, he had a warm regard—

a regard which never abated. He carried on his studies with unceasing perseverance. For one thing, he was, we should suppose, one of the best French scholars in England. He has preached in French to a Parisian audience. His first pastorate was in Willesden, where he established what is now a strong Presbyterian church. There he found a remarkable circle of intelligent and appreciative hearers. The congregation steadily grew, till after a few years he was appointed Professor of Hebrew in the Presbyterian College. While his academic tastes were decided, and his fitness for the position universally admitted, many regretted that such a man should be withdrawn from the pulpit. As a rule, the professor's birth is the preacher's death. For whatever reason, it seldom happens that the two functions are exercised together with real success in both. With him it was strikingly the reverse. His appointment as a professor was the signal for his emerging as a pulpit force of the first rank. He loved preaching, and freely accepted invitations to appear not only in the churches of his own denomination, but in other places, notably among the Congregationalists. His vogue steadily grew, till he became one of the most popular preachers in the country. The announcement of his name always brought together a great audience —generally as remarkable for quality as for quantity. At the same time he carried on with conscientious fidelity and unbroken success his work as a professor. To this he added literary engagements, and so his labours increased, while, alas! his strength did not. He was, in fact, one of the most prominent figures in the religious world of London, and the penalties attaching to such a position are terrible for a man in delicate health. The strain began to tell, but it was not easy to convince him of this. Latterly he became aware—very imperfectly aware—of his danger, and consented to limit his work to one sermon a week. But it was too late, and now he is at rest.

Our first thought and our last about him is that he was a Christian. He was a true believer. Whatever his doubts may have been, they were long gone. He knew, as few men know them, the difficulties of faith. In Biblical criticism he was a master, and he was very well abreast of scientific thought. But the problems thus suggested never threw one shadow on the clearness of his assurance. He held his faith with a certain large simplicity, but with absolute conviction. He dwelt in the positive. The truths on which his own life was fed, and which he ministered to others, were untouched by scepticism. Though he was a very brilliant and cultured man, with a wide range of interests, it is not of his gifts or his knowledge one thinks: it is of the deep Christianity which suffused all. It is impossible to imagine any one more free from cant; he gave himself a large liberty; he loved the 'innocent glories' of life, and was, when free from illness, very mirthful; yet, somehow, it was clear that for him to live was Christ, that he lived by the faith of the Son of God, that the Saviour was the Light of all his world.

His spirit as well as his faith was Christian. He owed much to nature. His winsome face, his gracious manner, his careful respect for the humblest, were born with him. He greatly resembled his beautiful and gifted mother, and as he lay in his last sleep the likeness was startling. But the unfeigned sympathy that dwelt in him could only come from Christ. The intellectual qualities of his preaching were less wonderful than its healing power. He would often earnestly say that his experience of life showed him that people needed comfort, and that it was in this way they were best reached. Scolding in the pulpit he abhorred, although he was accustomed to set forth duty incisively and plainly, especially the duty of making home bright. He not only met but anticipated calls for sympathy. He had a quick intuition of pain, and set himself to allay it. With doubters he was specially at home, and they with him. His correspondence with this class was very large and interesting. With the growing feeling that the Christian Church should care for the whole life of man he was in thorough accord, as his speech on Socialism at the Pan-Presbyterian Council showed, and he used to speak with great warmth of the noble work carried on by his neighbour, Dr. Clifford. Very little of his sermons was written. His mind was very fertile; he had always many subjects on hand. He was a very original preacher, and rarely read the sermons of others. His judgments were always charitable; he loved to look at all things from the point of concord; indeed, he was one who preached *peace* by Jesus Christ.

His more prominent work as a preacher must not be allowed to obscure his career as a professor. When his fever was approaching its worst, we received a letter from one of the most distinguished Hebraists in this country, in which he said Dr. Elmslie could combine brilliancy with exact knowledge in writing on Old Testament subjects better than any other living man. This is enough to show how faithfully he gave himself to his work. He had the two necessary qualifications for a successful professor; he was an exact scholar, and he respected his students. It is touching to see the dictionaries round his desk, and the traces of the study by which he was constantly widening his knowledge of Oriental languages. The work was very pleasant to him, for he loved to make things plain, and his pupils were loyal and diligent. His views on the structure of the Old Testament were largely those of the newer school of critics; but on important points (as, for example, the authorship of certain psalms) he dissented from them. Construction was more to his taste than criticism; and he drew a sharp line between critical theories and the inferences drawn from them. It is inexpressibly sad to say that his large plans of literary work are almost entirely unfulfilled. His great purpose was to write a book which should carry the message and meaning of the Old Testament to the people, and for this much needed service no one perhaps was equally qualified. He had completed notes on the Minor Prophets, which will be published; and we hope selections from his manuscripts will be available. He occasionally wrote in magazines and reviews, and one of his earliest papers was noticed by Professor Kuenen. To our own pages he was a frequent and much valued contributor. It is pathetic that his paper on 'Socialism' for the Young Men's Page was announced for this number. With his wonted consideration, he thought of this at the beginning of his illness, and said that all the materials were got together, if only he had the strength to write. The little notice of Tolstoi that appeared in our last issue, and the review of Lichtenberger printed this week, are his final contributions; and almost his last work was to correct the proof. He suggested for our Young Men's Page a discussion on 'War,' and wished to write something to prove its nobler uses. Of other plans and projects frequently discussed it would only be painful to speak.

If we venture to set down some recollections of many prolonged talks it is to break no confidence. The opinions are those he never concealed.

In theology he was always open to new light, always ready to add to his working stock old truths previously neglected. It is our impression that his preaching was growingly positive. He was much interested in discussing such books as Martin Luther on the Galatians, which show how the awakened soul is touched by Apostolic truth unmixed and unfrozen. What he specially disliked was bigotry. He would have sympathised with Robinson in his saying, 'When I see a spirit of intolerance I think I see the great Devil.' It was painful to him to be denounced as a heretic, and he showed himself hurt on learning that he was excluded from a certain place on account of his 'loose views.' Yet he endeavoured to find an excuse even for the most uncharitable, and he was grieved not so much by the suspicions of himself as by the mischief which he knew such persons did among the young and inquiring. There never was any one who less deserved to be suspected; he was no revolutionist, and was anxiously respectful of reasonable and even unreasonable susceptibilities.

While loyal to his own Church, and setting great store by the good-will of its ministers and members, he did not attach much importance to the barriers which divide it from the other Free Churches of England. Among the Congregationalists his preaching was very popular, and he was pressed to become Mr. Baldwin Brown's successor at Brixton, and later on to accept the pastorate of Westminster Chapel. The latter proposal we know was very seriously considered, and was not declined from any reluctance to enter the Congregational ministry. He used to speak very strongly of the old-fashioned genuine piety to be found among Congregationalists.

He thought the spiritual life of Nonconformity very deep and true, and was shocked by the recent attempts to make out the general apostasy of the Free Churches. He considered that the Congregationalists and the Presbyterians were destined to become one body. He often discussed the conception of the duty of English Presbyterianism advocated by some—to stand neutral in the great struggle and provide a place of refuge for the discontented in both camps. Politically, he was an ardent Liberal, and a thorough-going Home Ruler.

On no subject did he talk more freely and joyfully than on personal religion. He delighted to speak of the beauty of God in Christ, of His wealth of love, and especially of His readiness to forgive. The last long conversation we had with him was on the gospel of salvation to the uttermost; the magnificence of Divine grace; the hope set before the worst sinner of welcome and pardon. No man was less of a pessimist. He took the most hopeful view of the future. He believed that God was leading the generations on, and had a buoyant assurance of the triumph of the Spirit of Christ. In this was involved the success of every righteous cause. These faiths and hopes sustained his clear spirit through his manifold labours, and his bodily sufferings. His health was never robust; it was at best never equal to the strain put upon it by his ardent mind. Latterly, we believe preaching was sheer poison to him. He strove to do his best, and now that he has finished his work and gone home to God, it is useless to question or repine. *Neither shall there be any more pain,* is a word much with those who knew at what cost his labour was wrought.

He was married about seven years ago, and leaves one child—a son. Of the faithful love that made him so happy, that watched over him with such jealous care, and which he recognised with the last sign of consciousness—of the grace and joy of his household, and of the desolation which has fallen on it now, we cannot speak. In him English Presbyterianism has lost its most brilliant and beloved member. The whole Christian Church asks the question put so continually and resultlessly—'Why was all this carefully, drop-by-drop collected store, precious beyond calculation, emptied on the ground?' We cannot answer one of a thousand, but our departed friend's abounding faith warns us not to charge God foolishly. It seems miserably selfish to speak of personal feeling, and yet there are many who would have rejoiced in his life and success more than in their own; who in many a heavy hour will remember the face which merely by its brightness used to lift the cloud; whose hearts will for long, at every thought of him, 'ache with all the past.' Only, 'they who love God never meet for the last time.'

November 22, 1889.

THE SCOTSMAN: DR. JAMES BEGG

When Lord Beaconsfield was introduced in Edinburgh to Dr. James Begg, he remarked to a friend, 'That is *the* Scotsman.' It might have been said with equal truth that the great ecclesiastic was a Tory democrat before the time. But little remains to justify the opinion of Dr. Begg's powers formed by many who knew him, and the biography just completed will do nothing to help in this. A fatality has attended the biographies of the heroes of the Disruption. With two or three exceptions they are deplorable, presenting the images of fussy, bigoted ecclesiastics, always making speeches or taking bitter part in petty quarrels, and completely dissociated from the larger world of culture. In comparison with Dr. Begg's life, however, the worst of them is a classic. Its one merit we are wicked enough not to appreciate. Everything is left out that could give pain to individuals. There was no doubt a good deal that might have been printed, for it was well known that Dr. Begg could on occasion, like Dandie Dinmont's terrier, 'behave himself distinctly.' The book is, in short, a heap of hay and stubble, with one or two needles hopelessly lost therein.

Nevertheless Dr. Begg was no small man. As a preacher he was not specially distinguished, though he was all his life a faithful minister of the New Testament, and lived in the hearts of his people. The peculiarity of his pulpit oratory was its abundance of Scriptural quotation, which he often used in an impressive and beautiful manner. He was no scholar—not even a man of wide reading—and he was wistfully aware of a defect which often laid him open to weaker men after the time was past for repairing it. He was almost invariably in a minority—a champion of lost causes—and though the ability of his coadjutors has probably been underrated, the leader was more than the army. He was generally in conflict with the tendencies of the times, and sometimes, we think, with the tendencies of the eternities. Yet he remains to us, after some observation of athletes in larger arenas, one of the most striking and memorable figures we have ever gazed on.

The life of the ecclesiastic is straining where strain is most dangerous—we mean morally. Some are called to it, however, and he was. To form a true idea of his great, eminent, and commanding gifts one had to see him in the Free Church Assembly. Mrs. Oliphant makes so much of 'a large presence,' 'a noble presence,' 'an imposing presence,' that one begins to think that the fit rulers of a distracted country are to be looked for in caravans. Still there is something in a stately presence, and Dr. Begg's noble and leonine face, his ample figure, his large and easy power, his soft yet strong accents, his genial humour, and his worldly wisdom made him one of the most pleasant and convincing of speakers. What made him great was that he had something of the old heroic strain, a kinship with those who loved not their lives to the death. His hearers would be still smiling at a racy story when or ever they were aware their souls were like chariots, and they were out on the moor 'wi' Richie,' signing Testimonies and Covenants in blood.

His contentions, so far as the outer husk of them is concerned, would now be anachronisms. His arguments on the sinfulness of 'human hymns' were many of them sufficiently preposterous. But can there be a greater loss than to disuse the record of that life that follows hard after God—its meetings and partings, its desires and hopes, its noons and midnights—which is written in the Book of Psalms? His ideas about the Bible, the Sabbath, and Popery may be open to much criticism. But are not the Bible and the Sabbath what he called them—the two great pillars of visible religion? Has ever religion flourished where the Book and the Day have been despised? And when all is said and done, is not Roman Catholicism a standing menace to our country? Dr. Begg interested himself much on social reform; he had a deep sympathy with the people, and especially for the oppressed and poor. When very near the end the imprisonment of the crofters began. Old and feeble though he was, he did not hang back:

> 'I was ever a fighter: so—one fight more,
> The best and the last.'

Even of his resistance to Disestablishment we may say that the vision before him, however impossible, was not ignoble—the vision of a holy church in a holy land.

Of his faults we have no mind to speak. We are all sinful and, generally speaking, fallible. Of accusers—candid friends and candid enemies—Dr. Begg had no lack. He felt what they said, and was touchingly responsive to any expression of kindness. But he could endure abuse and work without praise. That he was almost always on the unpopular side is proof, if proof were wanted, of his disinterestedness. It is a poor and shallow explanation of any forceful life that refers its main direction to small and personal impulses. He spoke not much of his religious experience, but it made him courteous in debate, patient in defeat, sustained him for years in heavy labours, under sharp trials, in long endurance of pain. Doubtless his life was hid with Christ in God. When he died the old words came to our mind—He hath delivered my soul in peace from the battle that was against me. He was taken away in time, for he had not the knowledge nor the training to cope with the new situation. When the conditions were changed, when the old axioms were disputed, when all was thrown into the crucible, it was fit that he should depart—'fit that in the fall of laws a loyal man should die.'

April 27, 1888.

DR. HORATIUS BONAR

Before the publication of our last issue, announcing the alarming illness of Dr. Horatius Bonar, the venerable poet-preacher had gone hence. His strength had been declining for years, and from Tuesday it was evident that the hand of death was upon him. So has ended a long life, eminently laborious, consistent, and influential.

Dr. Bonar, who had passed the age of eighty, was brought up in a cultured Christian home in Edinburgh, and came of a line of ministers. He was a diligent student, and a favourite pupil of Dr. Chalmers. Among his early associates were Robert McCheyne, A. N. Somerville, William Wilson, Sir Henry Moncreiff, and others—all of them remarkable, not only for evangelistic fervour, but for their devotion to theological scholarship. His first pastorate—which he occupied for close on thirty years—was in the beautiful Border town of Kelso, where his memory will long be cherished. There his activity knew no pause. What impressed every one was his unslackening toil. The light burned late in his study window; he was at his desk early; and as he was physically vigorous, and possessed of a resolute will, the work he accomplished was marvellous. He was continually preaching, and was as much at home in speaking to a little gathering at a cottage fireside as in any church. He was always writing. He edited many periodicals, and was chief contributor as well as editor: almost every year he published a new book, and he conducted a vast correspondence, for inquirers all over the world wrote to him. When he removed to Edinburgh he built up a large and influential congregation, and took his place as one of the foremost ministers of the city—continuing at the same time with almost unabated diligence his literary labours. We doubt whether many have put more of sheer toil into their days, and happily his days were not few. And all his labour was devoted to one purpose, for from end to end of his career he was true to his early principles and convictions, never leaving the standard he had raised and gloried in from the first.

His was an eminently influential life. Even if he had not been a sacred poet Dr. Bonar would have been distinguished. He was a scholar, a thinker, a devoted lover of books, which he amassed in vast numbers, paying, we are bound to say, more reverence to the inside than the outside. Indeed he was imbued with that noble passion, the *amour antique des lettres humaines*, and we are persuaded he would have sympathised with the illustrious French orator who, near the end of a toilsome public career, confessed that the dream of his whole life had been that of writing for God and for souls. The influence which his books had among English Nonconformists is witnessed to by Dr. Dale; for whom, by the way, he had much regard. But in the Church of England—the evangelical section—it was far stronger: few names stood higher than his. We have said nothing of Scotland and America. But, as it happened, the literary productions he least thought of were by far the most popular. These hymns were ushered into the world in the most unpretending manner. Some of them were printed as leaflets, to be sung by the Sunday School scholars in Kelso; others were used to fill up vacant spaces in the *Quarterly Journal of Prophecy*. He wrote some of the best known in railway carriages, and some when sitting for a brief rest by the fireside after a day's work. They have gone round the world, have been sung in churches of all communions, have been learned by little children, and hung as lights over the thickly closing waters of death. It is significant of Dr. Bonar's strong conservatism that he had never had these or any other hymns sung in the churches where he ministered till a very few years ago.

It is from these hymns and his other poetical works—notably, 'My Old Letters'—that he may be best understood. They show, to begin with, unmistakable poetic genius: perhaps he has hardly had full justice done him in this respect. A quiet refinement of taste reigns everywhere; the colouring is chaste and beautiful. The lines of thought are very simple, and the expression not less so, for he hated obscurity. One class of hymns states with perfect lucidity the main facts of the Gospel; the rest may be termed hymns of homesickness. Through these latter there sounds the refrain of 'the solemn canticle of death.' The very first of them runs thus:—

> 'Not first the glad and then the sorrowful,
> But first the sorrowful and then the glad;
> Tears for a day, for earth of tears is full,
> Then we forget that we were ever sad.'

The pleasures of the world are delusive:—

> 'Now a stranger
> I pass along the smiling earth;
> I know the snare, I dread the danger,
> I hate the haunts, I shun the mirth.'

The world lies in wickedness; its princes have set themselves against our Lord and His Christ; the Church, a little flock, waits and weeps under 'the still unrended skies.' There is a great deal in the 'Hymns of Faith and Hope' which recalls the temper of 'Lyra Apostolica.' Thus in the hymn, 'A Little Flock,' where we read—

> 'A little flock; so calls He thee:
> Church of the firstborn, hear!
> Be not ashamed to own the name;
> It is no name of fear.
> Thy words among the words of earth,
> How noiseless and how low!
> Amid the hurrying crowds of time
> Thy steps how calm and slow!'

we cannot but think of—

> 'Bide thou thy time,
> Watch with meek eyes the race of pride and crime,

Sit in the gate and be the heathen's jest,
Smiling and self-possest.
O thou who promised art the victor's sway,
Bide thou the victor's day!'

Life is so full of temptation that it should be solemn 'as march of mountain streams.' It is so full of loss and pain that the clods of the valley are sweet as the place of escape and hopeful rest. He rejoices that time is passing:—

'Well pleased I find years rolling o'er me,
And hear each day time's measured tread;
Far fewer clouds now stretch before me,
Behind me is the darkness spread.'

It is nearly thirty years since he wrote on the birth of his son:—

'My flowers have faded, and my fruit
Is dropping from the tree,
The blossoms of the golden year
Are opening all on thee.
My harvest, with its gathered sheaves,
Is almost over now;
But thine is coming up, my child,
When I am lying low.'

And it is nearly fifty years since he wrote a precept some will remember at this time:—

'Let our farewell, then, be tearless,
Since I bid farewell to tears;
Write this day of my departure
Festive in your coming years.'

Even the brightness of his verses has something sombre in it, like the red flashing of a November sky. In a world where death and change will not suffer us to love in peace, and where the most faithful workers often sow in tears, such strains will always be caught up hungrily.

We have left ourselves no space to speak of Dr. Bonar as a preacher and as a man. His sermons were terse, authoritative, clear; as a rule not ornate, though the poetry at times would not be kept back. He once remarked to the writer that his favourite preacher was Harrington Evans, and there is a considerable similarity in their styles. He was a most winsome preacher to children. As a man, he was full of faith and prayer—of warm affections, strong friendships, generous in his gifts, and faithful to his convictions. No one who knew him could doubt that he was one of that high company who seek to measure all things here by the measure of Jesus Christ.

August 9, 1889.

BISHOP LIGHTFOOT

THE death of the Bishop of Durham was hardly unexpected. He had been prostrated by a long and distressing illness, from which at one time he did not expect to recover, and although strength partially returned, the serene loftiness with which in his latest speech he referred to death was almost prophetic. During these last months his hand was constantly at his work. He revised with amazing thoroughness his great edition of *Ignatius*, and prepared for publication his essays on *Supernatural Religion* and the Gospel of St. John. In these he delivered final and weighty testimony to central truth. Thus having done much service to God and man, having received such acknowledgments and rewards as man could give him, he has passed away in the fulness of his years, with his house set in order.

Bishop Lightfoot was pre-eminently the scholar of the Church of England, and as such found his first sphere of influence among the students of Cambridge. There is a characteristic theology of Cambridge, as there is of Oxford: Julius Hare is, in measure, to the one what J. H. Newman is to the other, whether acknowledged or not. But while no successor has arrived to divide the field with Newman, Hare has been almost forgotten in the living and masterful energy of such teachers as Lightfoot, Westcott, and Hort. Of these Lightfoot was unquestionably chief. His university career was one of nearly unique distinction. This fact of itself made him influential with young men, to whose favour intellectual power is essential, and who appreciate the certificate of university distinction beyond any other. With them, earnestness and piety standing alone go for nothing. But when goodness is joined to knowledge it counts for much; and when these are crowned by spiritual power paramount influence is the result. Lightfoot had all three. A scholar of the first rank, a man of transparent and genuine goodness, he was something more: a common-sense Englishman, reticent as to spiritual experiences, his face was pale at times with a light not of this world.

Bishop Lightfoot, indirectly rather than directly, did a work of far-reaching import in his own Church of England. The ingenious person who divided that communion into Low, Broad, and High, has been the author of much confusion. It never was a satisfactory classification; now it is hopelessly inadequate to cover the facts. Dr. Lightfoot could not be limited by any of these names. In the sense that he believed in the place, the greatness, and the mission of the Church of England, he was a loyal and devoted Churchman. He had no shrinking from comprehension, and in that sense might be termed Broad. Some of his chief friends (like Dr. Liddon, to whom his work on Ignatius is dedicated) were High Churchmen, and he, like his predecessor, the author of the *Analogy*, seems to have favoured elaborate services. He never entered into direct conflict with any party in his Church, and was as free from coveting any party name as Dean Vaughan himself. But his work was of incalculable significance for the future of Christendom. It was he who dealt its death-blow to the doctrine of Apostolical Succession as held by the mass of the High Church clergy. There is an increasing consciousness of this among them. Although they are not superior in theological learning to other divisions of the Church of Christ in England, they know in their heart of hearts that they must abide by the verdict of scholarship. And since we have witnessed Pusey's characteristic doctrine rejected openly by the head of the Pusey House, we need not despair of seeing the chief bar to Christian union taken out of the way.

Bishop Lightfoot, perhaps, did more for those outside as a defender, than as an expositor of the faith. Few will recollect Dr. Samuel Brown's first booklet, in which he took the *nom de plume* 'Victorious Analysis.' That has often struck us as very prophetic of scientific hopes. Science hoped to be 'victorious' by 'analysis.' Analysis was carried far, but the wiser leaders have always been aware that the Gospels must be analysed before any real triumph can be claimed. In this they had chiefly to reckon with Lightfoot, and a very serious business they found it. To many it was assurance and comfort that such a man championed the faith. It may be a very poor argument to say 'The President of the Royal Society is a Christian: therefore I may safely be a Christian,' but such as it is it goes far. But those who wanted more were not disappointed. The unfortunate man who was too easily persuaded that he had made an end of supernatural religion was taken in hand by the Bishop and hewn in pieces. The lowered and abated tone of scepticism in our day, and the confidence of Christian apologists, is largely due to this victory. Among scholars it was acknowledged that Lightfoot knew more of the early Christian literature than any other man. There are more brilliant men left even in his chosen field than he was: Harnack is a conspicuous instance. But it was hardly possible that he should be surpassed in actual knowledge. He began early, he lost no time, he took the right way, his mind was at once retentive and eager, he never printed anything to which he had not given the last finish, and never discussed subjects he did not perfectly understand. So even the Germans came to recognise that they had no man quite his peer. The sobriety of his judgment, if it had stood alone, they might not have appreciated. If you call a young Dutch New Testament critic wrong-headed, he may reply that you are dull. But when you can point out that your opponent, though he has the advantage of not writing in English, is only an amateur, something is accomplished. It is true that Lightfoot was not a great genius. He was not one of those interpreters in whose presence darkness readily breaks away. He does not yoke himself with the mind of St. Paul. But for certain permanent qualities of wisdom, knowledge, and thoroughness, he is unsurpassed among New Testament expositors, and we deeply regret that he has not been spared to accomplish the next labour he had proposed to himself—a commentary on Ephesians.

Of his work as a bishop not much need be said. Many not of his own communion grudged him to work so largely mechanical, but since he had to be a bishop, we regret that he did not die Archbishop of Canterbury. There is a generous instinct in human nature whereby we fancy that our great and wise are capable of anything; that they can overstep the inexorable *moenia mundi*; that the scholar can go forth into the world and guide it with his counsel. It is not so. Lightfoot did his best: his impulses were noble and generous; he longed to see the great salvation; he was full of the hopes that lift our fallen life; he never feared new ideas and new movements. He saw that something must be done—done at the risk of mistake—and he did it. But we are most attracted by the signs of a lofty and austere piety which mark his episcopate as they did that of Joseph Butler. Many viewed with misgiving the ascetic life of the author of the *Analogy*, his melancholy forebodings, his solitary habits, the ornate chapel where he bowed before a silver cross. Lightfoot's piety found, perhaps, more legitimate channels of expression, but it was of the same type—lonely, intense, and pale. In this lies his chief, his true greatness: that *Ad Te quacunque vocas* was his guiding rule of life.

January 3, 1890.

JOHN HENRY NEWMAN

> 'Be it mine
> One law to cherish and to track one line,
> Straight on to heaven to press with single bent,
> To know and love my God, and then to die content.'

THESE lines, from one of his least known but most characteristic poems, were written by Dr. Newman at Oxford in 1834, and on Monday evening their last aspiration was fulfilled. He died at the Oratory, Birmingham, after a short, sharp illness, a quarter before nine. Since the news came to them some of his readers have been haunted by these and many more of his own verses. Here is another, written in 1849 :—

> 'One moment, she said,
> And the dead will revive ;
> The Giants are falling,
> The Saints are alive.'

And *The Dream of Gerontius* comes up in pages for which we have no room. How is it with him now that he has met the burning and transforming flame of the Everlasting Love ? He has passed in silence, as Faber prayed he himself might, with no brave words on his lips. It has not been granted him to die like his hero, of whom we are told that on the day of his death he sang the whole of the *Gloria in Excelsis* with unusual joy and devotion.

But he died, as he had lived, with the humility and trust and sweetness of a child.

The external events of Dr. Newman's life are soon dismissed. He was born in 1801, in the City of London, and was brought up under evangelical influences, and with many opportunities of various kinds. His religious bent and intellectual power were soon evident. Though he failed to take a high degree at Oxford, and was never an exact scholar, his superiority easily made room for him. In 1822 he became a fellow of Oriel and an associate of Whately, now little more than a name. From 1826 to 1831 Whately's hold over him was gradually relaxed, and he came out as a leader of the new High Church party, and the most influential preacher Oxford has ever known. As author and editor he was incessantly active, and in February, 1841, he published the memorable *Tract Ninety*. In 1843 he retracted all his hard sayings against Rome, and on October 18, 1845, Father Dominic, the Passionist, came to him through the stormy rain in his retreat at Littlemore, and received him into the Church of Rome. Almost on the same day in the same year Ernest Renan quitted the seminary of St. Sulpice, and definitely withdrew from the clerical career. Since then with little interruption Newman has been at the Oratory, Edgbaston. For five years (1852-1857) he was Rector of the Catholic University in Dublin. The main events in his career were the Achilli trial, when he was prosecuted for calling a converted Romish priest a sensual apostate; his controversy with Kingsley, which ended in the publication of the *Apologia*; and his elevation, in 1879, to the dignity of a Cardinal.

It is as a preacher that Dr. Newman will live, and his power as a writer and speaker of sermons cannot be considered apart from his convictions, his character, and his literary power. He almost owed his soul to that great saint and doctor of the evangelical party, Thomas Scott, the commentator, for whom he had a lifelong reverence, shared by Mozley. The real peril of the soul, its preciousness, the terror of the sinner's future, were at the base of all his thought and action. He had also, in unequalled degree, that conviction of the real weakness of wrong and untruth for which men in all ages have fled to the sanctuary of God: 'The Giants are falling, the Saints are alive.' It is impossible to say how often, how sweetly, how victoriously, that note is struck through all his works. Then he had amazing acquaintance with the English Bible, from which he quoted lavishly, and often with striking effect. He must be a very dull preacher to whom Newman's collocations of verses have not furnished many discourses. Above all, as Dean Church says in his memorable estimate of Newman's preaching, an estimate never likely to be excelled, he made the sermon an 'earnest letter'—a call which came home to each hearer—a summons to ascend. And with him the heights of religion were very high.

The praise of Newman's style has become

sickening in its iteration, and the clumsiest provincials have been noisiest in laud. We need only say that in its music, sweetness, and combined passion and reserve it remains alone. What needs emphasising is that Newman was first of all a writer of sermons. His oratory had its own peculiar and holding charm, but he was not an orator. He read his sermons to an audience he respected. The many sermons which he preached extempore as a Roman Catholic were utter rubbish in the judgment alike of himself and his hearers. With a pen in hand he could do anything. And one touch of his poetry was more potent than all the unreserve (to use no harsher word) of Manning and Faber. These were great men (Newman himself used to put Manning at the head of English preachers), but they are not to be named with him.

His romantic character went far in explaining his influence. His delicate literary criticisms, as well as subtler indications, show how his spirit was cradled in romance, and there was always about him something high, chivalrous, daring, uncalculating. From the first he showed himself willing to surrender all things for a certain inner harmony, and in this high strain his long life was spent. He was never rewarded vulgarly; he never waxed gross, he never underwent the disenchanting processes of domesticity; he was always poor—even his great popularity as an author did little, we believe, to enrich him. And he had what Matthew Browne, after asking pardon of 'your sacred office, your spotless life, your grey hairs, and your transcendent genius,' calls the honour of an English *lady*. He defended his character with extraordinary passion. Had Kingsley kept away from that, Newman would never have paused in the midst of his solitary labours to turn aside and smite him. His wrath was kindled in the same way at Dr. Fairbairn. Indeed, this made him unconsciously very unfair. He always tried to make every controversy turn on his own sincerity. Of course he had an easy victory when it came to that, but we believe that the calm judgment of history will condemn him for having in more than one instance made a personal question of a far older and wider struggle.

His career as an ecclesiastic it would take a volume to describe. Much has been written about the Oxford movement, but its true history is untold. It has been obscured and perverted in cloudy reminiscences. The student will do well to study the Letters of Canon Mozley for sound ideas, and to follow them by a careful perusal of the pamphlets and periodicals of the time. He will then be in a position to sift the voluminous literature. Of the Church of Rome Newman was a sincere adherent. It is natural that his position should have been somewhat misunderstood. He could not swallow everything with the voracity and noisy relish which came natural to others. And when questions were stirred he did not raise the objections which would have occurred to a born Catholic: the leaven of Protestantism unwillingly asserted itself. We need not wonder, therefore, that he finally found silence best. And he was more accessible to Anglican and Dissenting ministers than to those of his own Church: they understood his past. Much might be written on this: we content ourselves with one instance. He used to speak with gratitude and affection of George Dawson, the reason being, we believe, that Mr. Dawson spoke up for him and defended him against prejudices, when he first came to Birmingham. Such things he never forgot. He was a most gracious and assiduous correspondent, and a proper selection from the immense mass of his letters should be an English classic. When strangers of other churches sent him their books, he did not put them off with formal acknowledgments, but found time to read the volumes, and commend them if he could. But of his countless deeds of charity volumes might be written. Of the spirit of his life and thought—sensitive, yearning, lifted up to God—a picture hung in his room at the Oratory impressively spoke. It was a view of Oxford, on which he had written, *Fili hominis, putasne vivent ossa ista? Domine Deus, tu nosti?* Son of man, can these bones live? O Lord God, Thou knowest.

August 13, 1890.

A DEBTOR TO THE WISE: DR. LIDDON

THE death of Canon Liddon is an unspeakable loss, for he was beyond dispute master of what Gratry calls the greatest of all arts, that of preaching. No man in England drew vaster audiences, and he attracted the educated classes as popular preachers very seldom do. When St. Paul proclaimed himself a debtor to the wise and to the unwise, he drew an enduring distinction. The greatest separation is the separation between minds. While Dr. Liddon neglected no part of his mission, he was specially called to the 'wise.' Among his congregations were always to be seen many of the guiding intellects of our time; and he had unique success with the most difficult of all audiences—educated young men. He realised his gift; he coveted the great office of prophecy from the beginning of his life, and worthily fulfilled it.

In exploring the sources of his vast influence we say nothing of his physical and intellectual gifts, or of those qualities of temperament which in him were equally marked. The dullest could not miss them, and the most richly endowed might covet them. You could not hear him five minutes without perceiving that he was not a philosopher, not a speculator, but a messenger and proclaimer.

'The Word of the Lord came unto me, saying,' might have prefaced all his utterances. He delivered what he had first received. One of his favourite expressions was that the truth of the Gospel was a truth that knew its frontiers. Haziness in religious teaching he earnestly deprecated. Why should it be esteemed a merit in that field, when in every other department men sought to get rid of it? According to his belief, God has made His will plain. He has not given a revelation of mists. If He had not answered the petition of His children for the solid bread of truth with a stone, He had certainly not met it by giving them a transcendental vapour. Dr. Liddon considered undogmatic religion insufficient for earnest moral struggle. For mere criticism he had no enthusiasm. It might do service by burning up the brushwood on the soil of truth; but the soul could live only on the positive. We cannot but think that this clear and ringing assurance went far to account for his success. It lulled the critical faculty of his hearers. So long as men listen to speculative guesses and arguments which have only the speaker behind them, they are vigilant and doubtful. But the man who disclaims all personal authority removes the great ground of quarrel. We may think that Liddon carried his dogmatism too far. From his sacerdotal and sacramental teaching we vehemently dissent, and he was too ready to make Christianity answer with its life for every one of his opinions. Sometimes he even seemed to fall into the dreadful error of those who talk as if it were possible that the discovery of an inscription, the digging up of a stone in Egypt, could separate them from the love of Christ. But his great strength was his undoubting faith in revelation. The critical intellect of the time will tear in pieces any of its own products—a religion as soon as anything. It is God who finds and chooses man. A god whom men find and choose is as much an idol as any work of wood and stone. *Show me the way in which I should walk*, is the prayer for a religion, and the answer is given when the heavens drop from above, and the skies pour forth righteousness.

Another chief source of Liddon's popularity with the educated was the large and grand commonplace in which he habitually indulged. Those familiar with the life and work of Lacordaire will be constantly reminded of him in reading Liddon. Lacordaire was, indeed, distinctly the deeper and the more powerful of the two. But his sermons, like Liddon's, contain much that is commonplace, and not a little that is rhetorical and fatiguing. The preacher who, generally speaking, admires freshness above all things is often disappointed with both. But with the hearer, however cultured, it is apt to be different. As Mr. Morley admirably remarks in his essay on Macaulay, 'The great secret of the best kind of popularity is always the noble and imaginative handling of the commonplace.' These words might have been written with an eye on Liddon's preaching. He too concerned himself 'with the perennial truisms of the grave and the bedchamber, of shifting fortune, of the surprises of destiny, and the emptiness of the answered vow.' He spoke of the great commonplaces—of God and sin, of salvation and redemption, of death and judgment; and, whatever his speech might lack, it was always informed by sincere and hearty faith. His preaching was also essentially addressed to his own time. He was keenly interested in all the movements of the day—an eager reader of newspapers; and his ambition was that of Hermann de Jouffroi—to pour a double portion of the gospel mind into all the laws and regulations of society. In doing so he never stood on the edge of the crowd as one in advance of the rest. His pulpit was lifted up in the very midst—the centre and the summit of the throng. But he was not always commonplace: he would not otherwise have reached his throne. Constraining is the charm exercised by those who can lead us, every time they preach, by untravelled lanes into unvisited nooks, who can show us some hidden spot in the mountains of truth that front us. But to many it is a greater thing when they see a new beam of light gild the solemn array. This his words did at times. In a sermon of which all the rest might seem ordinary there would be a sentence which woke the responses of the diviner mind, which revealed all the kingdoms of the spirit and the glory of them, which opened the eyes for ever.

Assuredly not the least potent of his spells was

his melancholy. In this too he resembled Lacordaire, from whose thoughts, even at their brightest, a tinge of gloom is never absent. The new leaders of High Churchism derive rather from Père Gratry in their hopeful outlook and their eagerness to face and overcome all the problems of their day. But to Liddon, as to Newman, the future of the Church often seemed dark. And the Bible does not tell us that Christianity is to go forward evenly, like a prosperous business growing every year. But Newman viewed the antagonism of the world as a war with the Stone which broke whatever fell on it, and ground to powder those on whom it fell. His well-known lines, 'Bide thou thy time,' are intensely characteristic. Liddon always grieved over the misery of the defeated, and the delay of Christ's victory. He discerned with equal keenness the sorrows of the individual life. His very clever colleague, Canon Scott Holland, published lately a volume with the title, *Christ or Ecclesiastes?*—a title which fairly indicates the present temper of preachers. Liddon would have said, and said truly, that the alternative was false: that Ecclesiastes is in Christ. It is not wonderful that the poor are carried away by the new gospel of sanitation, leisure, and comfort. But those who have all these are not deceived. They know that such things neither procure happiness nor detain it. For they do not abolish death. As the affections become more keen, as the vastness of knowledge grows, as wealth and luxury spread, the vanity of this life becomes clearer, and we look, according to His promise, for the new heaven and the new earth wherein dwelleth righteousness.

> 'And if that life is life,
> This is but a breath,
> The passage of a dream;
> And the shadow of death,
> But a vain shadow,
> If one considereth;
> Vanity of vanities,
> As the Preacher saith.'

Men who see through the shallow gospels of the hour give heed to the preacher from whom they learn to 'call their walls, Salvation'; who is to them the minister of an unseen hope. Such was Dr. Liddon to countless thousands of his generation. However divided from many of us by ecclesiastical distinctions, he was of those who in life and death acknowledge and adore Redemption: whose one hope is to be found with them of whom it is written, *Beati qui lavant stolas suas in Sanguine Agni:* Blessed are they who wash their robes and make them white in the Blood of the Lamb.

September 19, 1890.

A CHRISTIAN JOURNALIST: DEAN CHURCH

To many Londoners there is no sight in their city that compares with the dome of St. Paul's, rising mountain-like in size and perfect in symmetry over the agglomeration of buildings to which it gives character. But it is not even now what Sir Christopher Wren designed it to be. His idea of St. Paul's was that the stranger should enter it through bronze doors richly charged with Christian devices, and find himself within the walls of a glorious temple, pouring down upon him from every quarter a flood of soft, harmonious brilliance. What Dean Church tried to do for his cathedral, he and his early friends tried in measure to do for the Church of England—to give life and Christian solemnity to the cold and cheerless frame that waited for the inspiring breath. He has succeeded more largely than any other of the eminent men who have gone from us in recent months. Church left a school behind him. Newman, whatever he did for the Church of England, has done nothing for the Church of Rome. It pursues its dark track neither brightened nor altered by anything in his life and work. Liddon, in his last days, was a voice crying in the wilderness—almost terrified by the harsh echoes which came from the venerable Archdeacon of Taunton and other portents of theology. He died in solemn protest against the younger men of his school, to whom, nevertheless, he left the charge of his writings, and even in Keble College it seems impossible to secure the continued teaching of some of his most cherished convictions. Even in the case of Lightfoot, we doubt very much whether he will have successors after his own heart. The younger New Testament scholars are not quite on the same track. But Church was undoubtedly the father of the 'Lux Mundi' school, the strongest and most hopeful in the Church of England. They live to own their discipleship and to carry on his work. How did he gain this great, this enduring influence? Not by public utterances, for he never spoke from platforms, and his sermons—magnificent and indeed unapproached, as some of them are—were few, and delivered without oratorical aim or power. Not by personal intercourse on a large scale, for his life was secluded. Not by his books, for until quite recently these were little known, and they represent but a fractional part of his work. It was as a Christian journalist that he won and used to the end his immense influence. He had various journalistic engagements—some very important. But the chief was his connection with the *Guardian*, which he helped to found, to which he was a constant contributor, and by which in many anxious crises he virtually shaped the policy of the Church of England.

That such a man should have deliberately elected this use of his powers is an instructive fact. Whatley, of which he was rector during the best years of his life, is a very small parish near Frome. A hundred people might fill the little church, and almost all would be rustics. That the greatest Christian teacher of his generation found there an adequate sphere it would be absurd to say. He himself knew well how the English Church has failed to utilise the powers she possesses—he could point to men like Charles Cornish, one of the leaders of the Oxford movement—utterly thrown away in little dreary parishes. But he was satisfied at Whatley, and resolutely refused the most tempting offers of preferment. The Deanery of St. Paul's was literally forced upon him. For one thing, he loved the quiet, simple, homely life. Like his dear friend Mozley, he was very much at home with rustics. Both of them greatly admired the Rev. Samuel Rickards, of Stowlangtoft, a perfect type of a country pastor, shedding the light of an equable and happy mind on his neighbourhood, entering with whole-hearted sympathy into the life of his people, writing epitaphs for them in the village churchyard, and lying down by their side at last. Mozley, in one of his last articles, reviewed Mr. Rickards' *Poems*, which contain some of these epitaphs, and quoted, with special praise for 'its picturesque, plain-spoken simplicity,' this on 'William Street, a faithful and old servant of the Wilson family, in Stowlangtoft Churchyard':

'A heavy form he wore, combined,
However, with a gladsome mind.
Good friend was he, and free of speech
To all, with some glad word to each;
But oftener still in time of need,
He was the man for some kind deed.
His master he loved well, and knew
Full well his master loved him too;
And sooth to say, he looked like what
Belonged so wholly to the spot,
That now he 's gone all long to meet
Another man like William Street.'

It is significant that Church has chosen a grave in Whatley churchyard with his old flock. But undoubtedly his main reason for clinging to the little parish was that there he found the quiet, the leisure, and the detachment necessary for his labours as a journalist. Even when he came to London and the very highest place in the Church was offered to him, he abode as much as he could, and to the very last, by his old work. The only other religious journalist of the century who can be named with him—John Foster—whose work, curiously enough, was done in the same region—wrote sardonically in the *Eclectic* about reviewers doing their despised task in rooms whose 'windows were stuffed with old hats.' If the work is still lightly esteemed by some, it is well to remember that Dr. Church deliberately gave his life to it.

His power in all things came from his intense conviction and prophetic insight. On essentials his mind was made up. He quoted approvingly Bacon's saying that the Christian religion is the golden mean between the religion of the heathen, which left all to argument, and the religion of Mahomet, which interdicted argument. Dogma was a necessity of true religion. The Gospel was not a narrative with a supernatural fact in it here and there; it was a series of supernatural facts—the supernatural itself. For him wonders did not cease in the shadowy land of early history. He saw the angels of the sepulchre and the ascension flashing in upon a literary age and a period of effete civilisation. Nor did he make selections from the teaching of Christ. He accepted all; and recognised that Christ gave a new and more fearful sanction to law, and that chief points of His doctrine are the Last Judgment and Eternal Punishment. All theological progress was to him a more earnest study of the mystery of Redemption and the depths of the Divine Word. But this being fixed, he watched with eager sympathy the movements of criticism and science. He was ready, with a cheerful, bright-hearted acceptance, for all that was established. No one ever mistook him for a careless Broad Churchman. There are really religious men whose tone is not religious; but his theology had unmistakably the ideal element. And he had withal the rare and commanding prophetic quality. He watched the far-off horizon of thought, and was conscious of the coming clouds and the still more distant sunshine.

We have no space left in which to write of his very high, wide, and careful culture; of his style, which often had that last finish which accompanies exact and profound thought; of his love of beauty; of his intense moral glow. He could, and sometimes did, strike very hard—even savagely. It is curious to read the first form of his 'Anselm' in the *British Critic*, and compare it with that now in circulation. Matthew Arnold's books on religion moved him very deeply. Their insolence provoked him even more than their shallowness. 'So far,' said Dr. Church, 'as our observation reaches, Mr. Arnold has never displayed towards those from whom he differs seriously one grain of courtesy or respect.' In the last sermon he preached in St. Paul's (on Ascension Day, 1887 [1]), he unconsciously summed up his own experience. He spoke of the literature of Italy, in which he was so deeply read, as having for its master passion the love of beauty. 'Out of it arose, austere and magnificent indeed, yet alive with all instincts of beauty, the *Divina Commedia*, the mighty thought of Lionardo and Michelangelo, the pathetic devotion and deep peace of the Lombard, Tuscan, Umbrian schools; but to whole generations of that wonderful people—from the fresh sonnet writers and storytellers of the closing middle age, Guido Cavalcanti and Boccaccio, to the completest refinement of the days of the great Venetian masters and Ariosto—the worship of the beautiful, as the noblest, worthiest devotion, stood in the place of truth, of morality, of goodness, of Christian life.' He spoke of 'the

[1] Published, with notes, in the *Expositor*. Vol. vi. Third series.

spell and wonder of art and literature, the glory and sweet tenderness of nature,' as 'the brightness and joy of days that are now fast ending,' and of something deeper, more lovely, more Divine, for which the soul yearned—even 'the likeness in thought and will and character to the goodness of Jesus Christ.' For this he was always striving—now he has reached it in 'sinlessness, strength, peace, the vision of God.' It is this life-long quest which gives a peculiar force to the quietest parts of his writings. He glories when he speaks of what may be—of what has been. But when he speaks of what should be, it is a manner all the more impressive because low, gentle, and unshowy. He means more than he says; he unconsciously reveals how strong, strict, and severe was the discipline that governed his own life.

December 18, 1890.

CHARLES HADDON SPURGEON

WHILE the great congregations at the Metropolitan Tabernacle assembled on Sunday, their minister was lying unconscious at the doors of dawn. Ere the Sabbath ended he had passed through. The day for so long of his honourable toil was the day of his sacred rest—the day when he was gathered to the great host of his spiritual children who had gone before.

He has fallen like a tower, and his removal means for many a change in the whole landscape of life. A London Tory newspaper spoke of his death as attracting much less attention than that of Cardinal Manning. What did the children at the schools, the servants in the kitchen, the cottars in the Highlands, the old women in wretched garrets, know of Manning? But all these—all the nation, for the nation is Christian still—knew Spurgeon. In Scotland he was even more regarded than in England, and in America perhaps his fame stood higher than anywhere else. It is nearly thirty years since he said, not boastfully, but with perfect truth, 'Our word girds the world, and our testimony belts the globe.' His years were not many when he died, but he had lived long, and had maintained to the very last the splendour of his fame. Had Mr. Gladstone died at Mr. Spurgeon's age, he would by this time have been completely forgotten. Even as it was, Mr. Spurgeon was to many of his countrymen a still more conspicuous figure than Mr. Gladstone; it is not too much to say he was venerated beyond all other men.

The popular judgment is often mistaken; but it may be trusted to detect a charlatan *in time*. For the public ear, though easy to gain, is exceedingly hard to keep. It says much both for the power and the essential integrity of Mr. Spurgeon that he caught it when a mere boy, and never lost it for a moment. This was due first of all to his oratorical power. Two orators of the first rank have appeared in our time: Mr. Bright and Mr. Spurgeon. Spurgeon's marvellous voice, clear as a silver bell's and winning as a woman's, rose up against the surging multitude, and without effort entered every ear. The homely, sturdy Englishman, with his air of composed mastery, his unfailing command of lucid Saxon, his power to rise on occasion to the heights of eloquence, his compassionate understanding of the life of his people, and above all, his yearning for their salvation, will not easily pass from the nation's memory and heart. Mr. Spurgeon's almost supernatural keenness of observation was a great element of his influence. A well-known neighbour of his has never been able to recognise his members, because he cannot recall faces. It is not a fault; but it is a misfortune. Mr. Spurgeon at one time, as he sat on his platform, could name every one of his five thousand members. He also remembered even visitors with whom he had a very slight acquaintance; and when they came to the Tabernacle instantly detected them. He was pretty sure to contrive some way of making signs to them before the service ended—in manners sometimes quaint enough.

He was, however, much more than a great orator. The present writer, thrown on one occasion for six months where books were scarce, commenced to read a complete set of the *Metropolitan Tabernacle Pulpit*, and went through all the volumes. We can hardly imagine any one doing this without receiving a profound and permanent impression. More, the astonishing ability of the preacher is as marked as his eloquence and his sincerity. In this respect he has hardly received justice. Many talk still of his 'crab-apple fertility,' and compare him compassionately with such men as Liddon. In truth, there was no comparison; each excelled in his proper sphere. As an unprejudiced and competent critic, the Rev. H. R. Haweis, said many years ago, 'It is perfectly extraordinary how able and powerful the great Baptist can be within his very narrow doctrinal limits.' We do not think that he succeeded to any great extent outside of the sermons, although his *John Ploughman* publications contain much racy matter. In the sermons there are many passages which a really catholic anthology of English prose would not omit, and an informing spirit which hardly breathes among us now.

It may seem a hard saying, but it cannot be doubted that his theology was a main element in his lasting attraction. Why has Calvinism flourished so exceedingly in the damp, low-lying, thickly peopled, struggling regions of South London—where James Wells, an utterly uneducated man, and a Calvinist so high that he thought Mr. Spurgeon a dangerous heretic, divided the honours with his young neighbour, and had such a funeral as South London had never seen before? To begin with, all religions for the masses are essentially the same. A Roman Catholic theologian, Father Dalgairns, says: 'Go and preach your uncertain Hell and your obscure Atonement in the streets of our large towns, how many proselytes will you gain among the masses, the stench of whose corruptions goes up to heaven more foully every day? You tempt them by the dubious boon of a universal salvation, but in so doing you deprive them of the consolation of a Saviour.' Mr. Spurgeon always made salvation a wonderful, a supernatural thing—won through battle and agony and garments rolled in blood. That the blood of God should be one of the ordinary forces of the universe was to him a thing incredible.

This great and hard-won salvation was sure; that is, 'it did not stand in the creature'; it rested absolutely with God. It was not of man, nor of the will of the flesh. Mr. Spurgeon's hearers had many of them missed all the prizes of life; but God did not choose them for the reasons that move man's preference, else their case were hopeless. Their election was of grace. And as He chose them, He would keep them. The perseverance of the saints is a doctrine without meaning to the majority of Christians. But many a poor girl with the love of Christ and goodness in her heart, working her fingers to the bone for a pittance that just keeps her alive, with the temptations of the streets around her, and the river beside her, listened with all her soul when she heard that Christ's sheep could never perish. Many a struggling tradesman tempted to dishonesty; many a widow with penury and loneliness before her, were lifted above all, taught to look through and over the years coming thick with sorrow and conflict, and anticipate a place in the Church Triumphant.

There is a very prevalent notion that the doctrine of a universal Fatherhood as often preached, springs from a truer charity and is more comforting than the old way of teaching that God is the Father of His children through faith. A man says, 'God is the Father of the East-end of London,' and thinks he has uttered a consoling truth. What Mr. Spurgeon felt was that the Fatherhood of God must mean a great deal more than that. In a sense God is the Father of the most degraded, but what does that come to? Before we know the Fatherly nature the Son must reveal it, and if we dare to say it, there is something beyond that. The going out of the Divine Heart to poor, lost, guilty creatures is an expression of the lower deep of love in God's own being, and means something—means everything for as many as receive it. It is not the cold comfort, the unsheltering shadow of an empty phrase.

The very poor—it must be remembered that South London is the poorest part of the metropolis—are beginning to hope that councils and parliaments will do much for them. They may find it so, but Mr. Spurgeon made little of such things. He taught them—the staple of his sermons is—that now, in the living communion of the soul with Christ, they might have all the joy they needed. A man too wise, too experienced, not to know how slowly the battles of the poor are won, and how little their victories often yield—he insisted on the joy and peace in believing, which the world could neither give nor take away. Life might pursue its hard, monotonous way of obscure toil, scanty wages, and a great weight of care, but over it all there might rest a soft and sacred light. The common people heard this gladly, and well they might, for it is so. Perhaps when they have had a little more experience of the politician they will hear it more gladly than ever.

Personally Mr. Spurgeon was keenly alive to the humorous side of things—witty, brilliant, and sometimes exuberant. But as is so often the case with such natures, his thought turned habitually to the wistful, pathetic, melancholy side of life. George Herbert's lines fitted him well :—

'Not that he may not here
Taste of the cheer,
But as birds drink and straight lift up their head,
So must he sip and think
Of better drink
He may attain to after he is dead.

'But as his joys are double,
So is his trouble;
He hath two winters, other things but one;
Both frosts and thoughts do nip
And bite his lip;
And he of all things fears two deaths alone.'

In manner he was scrupulously and even anxiously courteous. For long he mixed little in society; he was busy with his tremendous labour, and incessantly occupied in reading. He had a great collection of commentaries arranged in order round the walls of his sanctum, and never preached without consulting each on his text. Though his habits of preparation were peculiar, they were thorough and exact. Never did he trifle with the chief duty of his sacred office.

But we must leave many things unsaid. Never has a man with such an experience appeared in the Christian Church—never one who has addressed so many of his fellow creatures on the things of God—never one the obvious results of whose ministry have been so great. 'I shall never hear you calling,' we say as we think of that unforgotten voice. But its echoes will linger when the strife of tongues is passing. Multitudes will think with affectionate and respectful sympathy of the bereaved wife and sons, and of the great church over which he presided. We have all lost much, but he has gained more. His was a nature little fitted for many things that befell him in the last lacerating years —less fitted still for the long inaction which was the best his physicians dared to hope for. Better for him, better, perhaps, for us, that he has gone up the shining road.

February 4, 1892.

DR. ANDREW BONAR [1]

It is but a year since Dr. Andrew Bonar passed silently and gently within the veil. Almost to the end of his long life his ministry continued. He was not withdrawn by bodily infirmity as one shut up in Israel, and although the marks of old age were upon him, his spirit was entire and unwearied to the very last. His ministry has been speedily renewed by the publication of his diary and letters —a book of which it is the best commendation to say that it recalls the writer, so that in every page one seems to see and to hear him again. Miss Bonar has done her work with rare wisdom and grace. There is not a line in the volume that we should like to see left out. The editor contributes little, but that little is of the best sort. This is perhaps the most impressive Scottish religious biography that has appeared since Dr. Bonar's own Life of McCheyne was published, and we cannot but think that it will deeply move many readers. For while it is true that the testimonies of those who have lived and died in the faith and fear of God are always precious to the Church, there is something peculiarly helpful in the witness of

[1] *Andrew A. Bonar, D.D.* Diary and Letters. Transcribed and edited by his daughter, Marjory Bonar. (Hodder and Stoughton.)

Andrew Bonar. When the world closes on us, when we are strained by the bustling, overwrought tension of the time, when the unlovely toils of working life are too much, it is good to pass into the peaceful atmosphere of this book. It should make its readers gentler, humbler, more faithful, and more patient. It breathes the living spirit of the Apostolic Church. It is a great testimony to the reality and richness of that spiritual life which is still bestowed by Christ. We can hardly imagine any Christian reading it without being shamed, or rather won, to greater earnestness, without feeling the power of the love which burned in the heart of the writer. Let those who think we have praised this book too highly read it; they will not think so then.

Andrew Bonar was born in Edinburgh in 1810. His father was a man of position and culture, and the boy became a distinguished student. Without doubt Andrew Bonar was the best Latin scholar who ever passed through the hands of Dr. Carson, the Rector of the High School. At the University he took one of the highest places, but from the beginning religion was his chief concern. Along with his brothers John and Horatius he attended the prophetical lectures Edward Irving was then delivering at half-past six in the morning. The three young men accepted the premillenarian view, and maintained it through their long lives. Horatius Bonar became known to all the world as a hymn-writer; John Bonar was a magnificent preacher; Andrew's career is told in this book. They all reached their ministerial jubilees; and two of them, Horatius and Andrew, became Moderators of their Church. There was a singular harmony between the three; though their temperaments were dissimilar. Andrew Bonar was certainly not the least gifted. Though he never wrote verse, his sermons often shimmered with poetry. He was of scholarly habits, familiar with the original text of Scripture. But his winning, quaint, and beautiful personality was his chief distinction; and this diary helps us to understand it.

After a probationary period, Mr. Bonar was settled at Collace, a country parish in Perthshire. There he remained for eighteen years. There are signs that he himself wondered somewhat at this long seclusion. At an earlier period he writes, 'Greatly cast down by the circumstance of my being kept out of several appointments, on account of my millenarianism chiefly. I had prayed about the matter in the full conviction that bearing testimony to this and other truths was the path of duty.' But he humbly accepted his place. Even during the early part of his ministry his spiritual power and genius were recognised by some discerning hearers through the country, and he had a scattered but enthusiastic band of admirers. He was the closest friend of McCheyne, and wrote a biography of him which has taken its place among religious classics. But we believe it is true that he was not valued at anything like his worth. For one thing, his millenarianism was curiously disliked; for another, his intellectual power was underrated. Even when at last he went to Glasgow, it was to one of the smallest of mission churches. We remember his saying that for a year his average congregation did not amount to two hundred persons. But he went on with his work, till at last he had a church membership of nearly eleven hundred, and was known for one of the most powerful religious forces in the city. When he had been there seven years, he sustained his great sorrow in the death of his excellent wife. Still uncomplaining, and blessing the Hand that smote him, he went on, amid signs of blessing constantly more clear. His existence came to be at last in the great, busy city of the West like the witness of a church spire pointing to God in silence, and his death was a bereavement not to a party nor even to a church, but to the devout and earnest among all classes of Christians.

Dr. Bonar's power, as this volume abundantly testifies, was the power of prayer. Again and again, from first to last, he tells us how for him the claim of prayer was supreme. 'Unless I get up to the measure of at least two hours in *pure prayer* every day, I shall not be satisfied.' 'I was,' he says in another place, 'living very grossly, labouring night and day in visiting, very little prayerfulness. I did not see that prayer should be the main business of every day.' In fact, this book is chiefly a testimony to the efficacy of prayer.

When we think of it, was not the apostolic life after the same pattern? Trace St. Paul through his life and writings, and do we not find everywhere prayer holding the first place? Indeed, the whole Bible is ringing with calls to prayer. His prayerfulness did not diminish—it greatly increased Dr. Bonar's activity, which was of the most amazing kind. His daughter does not say much of this, and she has done well. But his countless acts of ministration are known to Him who will one day declare them, for he never declared them himself. He descended upon his work, and so, while unresting, he was unhasting. There was a kind of still brightness about him when he visited. The work did not seem irksome; he did not need to watch for opportunities of spiritual converse; everything came naturally; his labours did not exhaust him, and the edge remained on his spirit.

His preaching was full of urgency. Earnestness about the truth is not the same thing as earnestness about souls. Perhaps there is as much desire to know and speak the truth as there ever was; but that which chiefly concerned Dr. Bonar was its effect on the people. He knew that the work of the Christian Church makes for the great ends of conversion and sanctification, and all his preaching was ruled by a desire for results. He mourned when he could see none. What really gladdened him was the news of souls awakened and confirmed, and when such tidings grew rare his heart was heavy.

One thing was always clear even to his humility. He never doubted his own free justification before God. 'I have many a time been unhappy for a season, but never led to doubt my interest in the Lord Jesus.' 'Went to sleep repeating "the Lord my Righteousness," and feeling as if with this upon my forehead I could go into the New Jerusalem and to the just.' The New Testament gave him the norm of the Christian life; and living in its atmosphere, he perceived that the experience even of great saints is often abnormal and morbid. His criticism of Brainerd in this connection is peculiarly instructive. Dr. Bonar held fast the great cardinal principles of the reality and necessity of the new birth, and the present acceptance and peace of all the justified. Profoundly conscious of sin and shortcoming, he would yet have said, 'Therefore, being justified by faith, let us have peace with God through our Lord Jesus Christ.' It is possible so to preach introspection and self-abasement as to belie the Gospel, and leave no place for the higher spiritual joys, and no ground for the offer of an immediate and transcendent blessedness. Whenever the spiritual atmosphere becomes clouded and gloomy, it ceases to be the atmosphere of the Epistles. There the triumph in Christ rises over even the great heaviness and continual sorrow of heart, the sense of sin and weakness, and the fear of being cast out at last.

Dr. Bonar's judgment of himself and his work was lowly, and he would have been the last to say that all men should be like himself. We remember well how generously he spoke of some whose conceptions and lines of service were very different from his own. There is all the more reason why his example should be closely and humbly studied. Those busy in the field are confronted by problems and situations in which they need resources he and his like did not possess. But reading this record, they will acknowledge that the ground-secrets of spiritual force were well understood by the father who is now at rest in the Lord.

December 7, 1893.

DR. ROBERTSON SMITH

PROFESSOR ROBERTSON SMITH succumbed on Saturday morning to his exhausting illness. The wonder is that he lived so long. He was afflicted with tuberculosis in various parts of the body, and had no illusion as to the course of the disease. For many months, indeed, he had been measuring its progress, exactly and calmly. He knew at least as much about it as his physicians could tell him. Yet with characteristic fortitude he continued the work and even the play of life—lecturing, writing, seeing his friends, and even occasionally travelling as far as London. Of late, however, the signs of the end were manifest, and he greatly contracted his plans of labour. His eager, restless, indomitable spirit is at last released, and has, we doubt not, found the Beatific Vision in the ineffable splendour of perfect knowledge, as well as in the opening of heaven and the Communion of Saints. When the tidings of his death came, some must have thought of Pattison's words about Scaliger: 'On the 21st of January, 1609, at four in the morning, he fell asleep in Heinsius's arms. The aspiring spirit ascended before the Infinite. The most richly stored intellect which ever spent itself in acquiring knowledge was in the presence of the Omniscient.'

We hazard very little in saying that Professor Smith, in the depth and range of his knowledge, had no equal among living men. Indeed, with the single exception of Lord Acton, none could be compared to him. As a Biblical scholar he stood among the foremost. He played the chief part in a great revolution of theological thought. His acquirements and achievements, however, will stand second, in the memory of all who ever knew him, to his strong and vivid personality. His was, in truth, a very precious and uncommon mind.

Dr. Smith's early years were spent in a country parish in Aberdeenshire, of which his father, a man of high scholarship and great mental force, was Free Church minister. It was a home where the severest intellectual discipline went along with warm family affections and earnest religious feeling. The minister had other pupils, but none within sight of his own sons. When the boys went to Aberdeen University, they speedily took the foremost place. One of them died early, after unexampled victories; the other, through ill-health, hardly reaped the full fruit of his toils. William Minto and William Robertson Smith divided the honours of these years. They were so greatly admired by their fellow-students that they were cheered whenever they stood up to answer a question in class. But one of their professors, still living, predicted that neither of them would reach the age of fifty, and the augury has come true.

Robertson Smith went then to Edinburgh, where

he acted for a time as assistant to Professor Tait in the class of Natural Philosophy, and studied theology at the Free Church College. His first paper was, if we mistake not, published in the *Proceedings of the Royal Society of Edinburgh.* It was an incisive criticism of some mathematical points in Mill's *Logic*, and was translated into French. Mill, in a letter we have seen, owned the justice of the strictures. Smith entered eagerly into the researches of Thomson and Tait, and his wonderful acquirements in mathematics are shown in the article on 'Numerals' which he contributed far on in his career to the *Encyclopædia Britannica.* But he was busy with other studies. He competed for the Shaw Philosophical Fellowship, and though surpassed by T. M. Lindsay (the winner) and W. A. Hunter—now well-known men—in acquired knowledge, his answers were considered by Professor Campbell Fraser equal in freshness and originality to any given in. He had found a more engrossing attraction in theology, particularly in Hebrew, which he studied under Dr. A. B. Davidson—a master whom he reverenced. In Germany he studied at various places—Bonn and Göttingen included—having among his teachers Kamphausen and Ewald. His amazing force and prodigious learning were fully recognised by the students, and he took a prominent part in the Theological Society, where he was known as the most formidable of critics and opponents. Among the recreations of that period was an article on Hegel's criticisms of

Newton, which led to a long and lively correspondence in an Edinburgh newspaper between himself and Dr. Hutchison Stirling. All this when he had hardly completed his twenty-second year!

Smith was twenty-three, and ready to be 'licensed' as a 'probationer,' when the chair of Hebrew in the Aberdeen Free Church College fell vacant. More than one qualified candidate entered the lists, but the extraordinary testimonials to learning and ability brought forward by Smith's friends conquered all opposition. 'Mr. William Robertson Smith, preacher of the Gospel,' was appointed to a theological chair over the heads of ordained ministers—a thing previously unheard of. He had given a specimen of his power in an article, 'Prophecy in the Critical Schools of the Continent,' which Dr. Allon inserted in the *British Quarterly Review*. The paper was rightly described at the time by Dr. Cheyne in the *Academy* as 'able; chiefly a vindication of Ewald's orthodoxy, and an attack on Kuenen.' It was read with admiration both by Dean Stanley and the late Dr. Candlish. The latter, however, saw that Smith did not believe in a single authorship of Isaiah, but was not greatly perturbed. At that time the Free Church was remarkably free from doctrinal controversy or alarm. The strong influence of the Disruption leaders—Cunningham especially—biased the most powerful minds of the Church in favour of orthodoxy, and they slept on as if drugged, while others around were wakening.

Dr. Smith commenced his work as a professor amid general hopefulness and goodwill. We remember, as if it were yesterday, his first lecture, delivered in 1870, when he was barely twenty-four. The subject was, ' What History Teaches us to Seek in the Bible.' His youthfulness, his extreme pallor, the abstruseness of nearly all he said, the ringing force with which he panegyrised Calvin and quoted from Luther, the pleased and puzzled aspect of the audience, and his own exuberance when all was over—these things are not easily forgotten. The lecture was afterwards published, and in the light of his teaching was not difficult to understand. It contained, indeed, the germ of what he held, if we mistake not, up to his death. There are in it the germs of a reconciliation between faith and criticism such as we feel, with sorrowful confidence, he alone could have worked out completely.

The young professor gave himself unsparingly to his work. His little band of students had the best he could give them. Even then his health was indifferent, and doubtless he overworked himself. He would come to his class often the very personification of weariness and exhaustion. But generally he revived as he poured forth the treasures of his thought and knowledge. His mental alertness and vivacity were, if possible, even more astonishing than his attainments. Books, instead of extinguishing, had kindled the flame of his thought. In private intercourse he was exceedingly communicative. The one subject on which he then had little to say was general literature. His work had left him no leisure for miscellaneous reading. Even in this department, however, Professor Smith was ahead of other men. He greatly astonished his students by a course of lectures on Hebrew Poetry. In these, though avowedly deriving in part from Ewald, he gave expression to most luminous and original speculations on the nature of poetry, and showed an intense appreciation of the literary beauty of the Bible. We remember the rapt expression with which he would quote such phrases as, 'The beasts of the field look up sighing unto Thee,' 'The fig tree standing white in the sun,' 'They were lovely and winsome in their lives, and in their deaths they were not divided.' He had some thought of publishing a book on Hebrew poetry, but contented himself with an article in the *British Quarterly*, which, though very good, omits what was most daring and distinctive in the original lectures. Personally he was very popular. Merciless in his criticisms, he often gave pain. He had little sympathy with slow wits, and none at all with anything else that might be pleaded in excuse for unprepared lessons or perfunctory essays. But though hasty, he was a man of warm, affectionate, and generous nature, and never provoked personal animosity. His critical position was at first somewhat conservative; thus he lectured on Egypt and the Books of Moses, following Ebers, and maintaining the antiquity of the Joseph narrative.

But he was of course far in advance of current Free Church opinion, and did not at first take all his students with him. Strictly conservative views were then powerfully represented in the Aberdeen College.

We pass with reluctance to the great controversy which divided his life—a controversy never to be thought of without misery, the most truly tragical episode in the church life of our times. Certainly the Free Church never had a more loyal and devoted son. Certainly no Church ever treated a young minister with greater confidence and affection. Yet the two were parted—to the great loss of both. It is the last thought in our mind to renew the battle over his grave, but we think English readers should know Smith's position, and that taken by the majority which removed him from his chair.

Professor Smith's critical views, which he first publicly expounded in the *Encyclopædia Britannica*, require no elucidation. They are those now taught by the Old Testament professors of almost every church. Theologically he taught the Reformation theology in its purity. Perhaps we may best summarise his views by saying that he insisted strongly on the personal character of revelation and faith. Revelation was not a supernatural communication of doctrine, but 'the direct personal message of God's love to *me*.' So the Bible was the actual realisation among men of a personal fellowship with God through word and faith. This it was in every part. Dr. Smith rejected the view that parts of Scripture are the Word of God and others not. 'People now say that Scripture contains God's Word, when they mean that part of the Bible is the Word of God and another part the word of man. That is not the doctrine of our churches, which hold that the substance of all Scripture is God's Word.' The silver was not in the leaden ore, useless to the man who could not smelt it. It was in a mould whose shape it took. 'The pure silver takes the shape of the mould, it may be an imperfect shape, but it is pure silver, and the man is enriched thereby without any further act.' It will be seen how on this view criticism was necessary and innocuous. It will appear also that the more rigid dogmatism of those who followed Calvin—Turretin, for example, down to Hodge—found little favour with Dr. Smith. He used to quote admiringly from Ames and others who recognised the personal character of revelation and the consequent need of a historical treatment of Scripture. But the Free Church as a whole accepted implicitly the theology of Dr. Hodge.

To understand his view of faith it was advisable to hear him preach. When his name as a teacher became famous through the land, great crowds used to attend his sermons. They heard nothing sensational; nothing personal; nothing extravagant; nothing that departed from the plain old lines of evangelical truth. Professor Smith preached the Gospel with such childlike faith and simplicity that only on reflection did men discover that his words, though clear as spring water, were as deep. He had the firmest grasp of the Reformation doctrine of justification by faith. Faith to him was not a function of the intellect assenting to higher truth than that of reason. It was a personal trust on God in Christ. 'The ground of assurance is nothing that is in us, but only the covenant grace of God and the saving love of Christ.' 'The covenant grace of God not resting on our merit, the saving love of Christ seeking the lost only because they are lost—these are what the Gospel holds forth as your warrant to come to Christ if you have not known Him before, to cleave to Him still if you have begun to doubt His grace.' He repudiated as vehemently as Maurice the title of a Broad Churchman. Of the Scottish Broad Church school he spoke with habitual contempt. His religion was 'churchly Christianity.' His views on the whole subject are set forth in one of the most valuable and characteristic of his writings, 'The Place of Theology in the Work and Growth of the Church,' published in the *British and Foreign Evangelical Review*. One of his own favourite expressions would have been eagerly repeated by Maurice—his assertion that it is not man who finds and chooses God, but God who finds and chooses man. It should be said that, in spite of the studied plainness of their style, his sermons contained passages of most marked spiritual beauty.

For the new views of the Old Testament the

Free Church was wholly unprepared. She had, indeed, been taught by her strongest and most revered men to look upon them as the result and sign of unbelief. If there was anything on which the Church prided herself, in which she was one, it was in the integrity and purity of her dogmatic faith. It must be owned that Dr. Smith, whose whole life and habits had been those of a student, very little appreciated the general ways of thinking on such subjects. It was not easy for him to place himself even where most of his brethren stood. At the time he first wrote he was a pioneer—much in advance of any recognised guide of the orthodox churches. Some of his most prominent defenders, indeed, pronounced his main conclusions false. The result was a grievous and prolonged controversy, in which the assailed professor showed the most brilliant ability. It was inevitable that little should be done to elucidate truth; much of the fighting was merely gladiatorial. The conviction gradually grew that Dr. Smith was a true son of the Church, one who threw passion into faith as well as into duty; there was an earnest desire on the part of many conscientiously opposed that he should be allowed to remain in his post, and the impression of his commanding intellectual power became universal. Indeed, he was actually reinstated, and had it not been for a new article appearing at a most unfortunate time, the controversy would have taken end. As it was, the majority of his opponents declined to pronounce his doctrines heretical;

they removed him from his chair on the ground that he needlessly disturbed the peace of the Church, but he retained his position as a minister. It was a great error, and he lived to see this owned on all hands. He saw the complete triumph of his long contending, though he had no share in the spoils. Views which seemed to many likely to pass like a summer storm, are now to all appearance permanently lodged in the Church. Some good may have come of the battle and its issue, for God knows how to use men's right-minded mistakes as effectually as He uses their right-minded service. But Smith's life was broken in twain: a great spiritual ministry was arrested in mid-course, and none of us may measure the loss.

We have neither the space nor the ability to write of Dr. Smith's subsequent career at Cambridge. His editing of the *Encyclopædia Britannica* was in itself a life-time's achievement. There was hardly any contributor, however abstruse his subject, who did not find that his editor could meet him on equal terms, and the marks of his hand are everywhere in that great enterprise. He became one of the most conspicuous and potent personalities in the University of Cambridge—influential in every sphere. It is deeply to be regretted that he was not spared to publish the concluding courses of his *Burnett Lectures*. The first, on the 'Religion of the Semites,' is an epoch-making book, and almost to the end he hoped that he might be able to prepare it for a second edition. In the other courses, as well as in the republication of his *Old Testament in the Jewish Church,* he showed that he had kept his early faith and bequeathed an invaluable legacy to the Church. It was to the Church and to Scotland that he belonged—so we shall always think. Whatever he accomplished as investigator or teacher in other fields, it was not by his own choice. He would fain have been in the Church—sharing its work of lifting the world to higher levels than those of time and nature. Like the Scottish metaphysician, Dr. Thomas Brown, in the words so beautifully commented on by Mackintosh, he chose to be buried with his kindred. The mind that soared and roamed over every region of knowledge, that measured itself unvanquished with the strongest of its time, turned back to the scenes and the friends of youth. He has been laid to rest in the Keig churchyard by the graves of his father, his brother, and his brilliant and beautiful sister.

April 5, 1894.

DR. R. W. DALE

On Wednesday of last week Dr. Dale succumbed to his long illness. He had suffered for some five years from a serious weakness of the heart, complicated by other troubles. His rallying power, however, was so surprising that there were strong hopes that his life might be prolonged. The end came somewhat suddenly about six o'clock in the evening. The news brought a great shock to those who were in any way associated with Dr. Dale, for the measure in which Dr. Dale was known was the measure of the love and honour with which he was regarded. He was so affectionate, so generous, so magnanimous, so true-hearted, so entirely forgetful of self, that he won the hearts of all associated with him. Into the sorrow of the family circle we may not enter. It is an agony which they and Christ must bear alone. But in time consolation will come to them from the thought that Dr. Dale died as he would have wished to die, among his own people, and that he passed away in the full height of an influence which was never so intense and pervasive as in the closing period of his life. The years that so often dull the will and contract the heart had no such power over him. Great as the grief of his church is—the church and people whom he watched over with unbroken solicitude and affection for more than forty years—that sorrow also has its alleviation. We are all of us grateful to God and to them that the bond between them remained unweakened to the last. The life now closed was not very long if counted by years, but measured by labour and conflict, it was far beyond the allotted age of man, and Dr. Dale so lived it that no Nonconformist of the century has left behind him a more splendid and stainless name.

Roughly speaking, Dr. Dale's life may be divided into three periods. The first was a time of preparation. Born in London in 1829, Mr. Dale at a very early period came under strong religious impressions. He tells us how, when a mere boy of fourteen, he read through Mr. Angell James's *Anxious Enquirer* on his knees, and in keen distress about his personal salvation. 'Night after night I waited with eager impatience for the house to become still, that in undisturbed solitude I might agonise over the book which had taught so many to trust in God.' The frank and instructive criticism of the *Anxious Enquirer* which appears in Mr. Dale's biography of his successor throws a strong light both on his theological convictions and religious experience. He looks upon the virtual identification of pardon and justification in that work as its great blemish. He argues that if the two are identified, the soul, when conscious of needing a renewal of pardon, will practically suppose that its justification needs renewal also; that it is standing in the same unsheltered and perilous position which preceded its original reconciliation to God. Any true theory of justification must leave that great and permanent blessing unaffected by the infirmities and sins which need daily confession and daily forgiveness. Mr. Dale held this view very strongly to the end. Two or three years ago he wrote us from Wales, speaking of his sleepless nights and the happiness which this glorious truth brought him in the silent hours. He had great delight latterly in the confirmation of his views which he found in Dorner's *History of Protestant Theology*. The point is one of cardinal importance. On it depends the whole temper of the religious life. If that is to be strong, buoyant, joyful, courageous, then the soul must not be thrown back day after day into the wretchedness and horror of being under the divine condemnation. With Dr. Dale to the very last the great characteristics of the Christian life were joy and courage, and notwithstanding his experiences of sorrow and weakness, he remained to the close not 'a miserable sinner,' but a hoping saint. It has been said that the whole basis of the Puritan character was a passionate, deep, religious organisation. This Mr. Dale possessed, but he would have laid even greater stress on the necessity of a definite and critical religious experience—an experience no less than the passing from death to life.

With this went the eager labour of a searching

and masculine intellect. There are souls, it has been said, and those among the noblest, to whom the primary avenue of access is the intellect, and who can only be led homeward by the illuminative way. The youth devoted himself to study at Spring Hill College, which he entered in 1847. Henry Rogers was then a professor, and Dale became one of his favourite pupils. His studies were crowned by two marked successes at London University. He won the prize for knowledge of the Hebrew text of the Old Testament and of the Greek of the New Testament. In 1853 he took the degree of M.A., with the gold medal in mental and moral science. About that time he was invited by Mr. Angell James to become his assistant in Carr's Lane. In November 1854, he became co-pastor, and for the succeeding four years, till Mr. James's death, worked with him most harmoniously and happily. On the death of Mr. James Mr. Dale became pastor, and his earliest literary work of importance was a biography of his late colleague. From the first, Mr. Dale held that the fervent spirit was not enough, that the prophet of power must be a thinker, and in easy command of the problems that agitate men's minds. But he did not immediately find himself, and we know that he afterwards discovered much to criticise in his earlier writing. The reward of his toil came in a very early maturity, and in a reputation and influence which soon spread themselves far beyond the limits of Birmingham.

The second part of Dr. Dale's life, which included the time when he devoted the whole stress and vigour of his amazing energy to innumerable labours as minister, as author, and as political and ecclesiastical leader, may be said to date from about the year 1865, or a little later. By that time his influence was commanding. His *Discourses Delivered on Special Occasions* had been reviewed in the *Contemporary* by Dean Alford, and had made him well known in the Church of England, as well as among Nonconformists. Through the twenty years of his magnificent prime his work was first of all ministerial. He was a true son of the Evangelical revival, a faithful preacher of the Christian redemption. His whole teaching rested on the truth that some have received the forgiveness of sins and others have not received it, and that every other distinction is insignificant compared with this. It was his practice to appeal to every hearer who had not repented of sin to repent straightway. He taught with uncompromising firmness that all needed conversion. He was wont to protest against the view that the poor and the vicious specially need to be preached to. That view, he thought, was held by men who regarded the Gospel as nothing more than a powerful agency for diminishing the perils of the State by reforming the dangerous classes of society. It did not trouble him that the respectable classes attended his church. He believed that the respectable classes needed salvation as much as any other.

He saw no clearer signs of the near approach of the millennium in the West End of London than in the East. He was aware of the dangerous force of unbelief among the cultured classes, and believed that it would be overcome by manifestations of the power and grace of God. To this is due his sympathy with the work of Mr. Moody and other revivalists. But Dr. Dale was not a mere evangelist. He was a great theologian, and his theology was delivered from the pulpit. He brought to theological study a highly trained and powerful intellect, a deeply religious heart, and a sense of literary form which made his work in that department of supreme importance. Dr. Dale's earlier writings are perhaps too diffuse. He had a picture of the particulars in his own mind, and incidents and allusions came to him in troops. His experience of life yielded readily a stock of instances on which he was wont to expatiate. But he tolerated no slovenliness or imperfection, and if at first he was too turgid, the study of the masters, especially of Burke, soon educated him to one of the most perfect styles in the whole range of English literature. A third and most important part of his pulpit work was his instruction on conduct. He held very strongly that the Christian ethic, which is the will of God, should be taught from the pulpit, and certainly no more effective moral teacher has ever appeared. This kind of writing he found very easy. Subjects and their treatment came without the slightest difficulty, while in dealing with the great truths that are the burden of revelation, he to the last experienced a certain sense of effort and strain.

Dr. Dale undertook and carried through almost incredible labours in the political and ecclesiastical world. Birmingham is a town which inspires its citizens with warm affection, and Dr. Dale threw himself without reservation into its abundant life. His services to the municipality, to education, to philanthropy, were countless, and can never be told here. No doubt his ecclesiastical and religious work gained from this contact with affairs. It has been said that no one would guess from Bishop Butler's writings that he ever had the disposal of five pounds. Dr. Dale was of another type. Full of sanguine energy and masculine activity, he knew too much about the sorrows of life to be overbearing. There was in him that moral thoughtfulness which Arnold made the goal of his teaching. At the early age of forty he became Chairman of the Congregational Union, and delivered the finest addresses ever given from that high position—addresses which he himself never surpassed. In the battle for religious equality he took the foremost place, and no such champion of the cause has appeared in this country. He had every qualification—firm principle, an entire freedom from the angularity of mind often seen in those who are brought up to object to what is established, a deep, steady undercurrent of strong feeling, and, above all, a religious temper which helped him to preserve a certain aloofness even in the thick of war. These twenty years were indeed rarely vivid, full, and happy. They were years when his only rest from work was in other work, and when he found that rest sufficient. They were years when he saw the fruits of his toil springing up on every side, and when it seemed as if he and the other captains of the Birmingham army were very soon to see the speedy triumph of every cause they pleaded.

Reverses came, and to those who do not know the facts it may have seemed that the last years of Dr. Dale's life contrasted somewhat sadly with the triumphant and thronged career which preceded them. But it was not so. By faith we understand that the dark Love which ordains our lot is wise, but sometimes gleams of light shine upon the way. It might have been said, it probably was said, that Dr. Dale had been too prosperous, too happy, too masterful. Hazlitt remarked that no woman ever cared for Burke's writing. It was too hard, too dry, too glittering. To Dr. Dale came, later than to most of us, the experiences of bereavement, sickness, and weariness, which test the reality of faith and the power of endurance. He encountered them bravely and tenderly. He was refined, ennobled, and taught by pain. It opened up to him such new reaches and depths of experience that he wittingly turned aside from many things that had claimed his care in order to develop the positive argument for Christianity, on which he had all his life relied. And so in him was fulfilled the great word that the men of sorrows are the men of influence in every walk of life. Not without tears was the New Testament written, not without tears can it be understood. In his earlier works Dr. Dale had consistently made his ultimate appeal to the experiences of penitents and saints. He came to see in his last years that he had been wiser than he knew. He came to see, and he was able to show, that the true verifying of Scripture lies in its application from point to point in life. This is the highest criticism, and it is a criticism which is independent of every other. 'They that wait upon the Lord shall renew their strength.' Is this true? If it is, then nothing else matters much any more. We behold as in a glass the glory of the Lord. So much every Christian knows. Is it true that, beholding, we are changed into the same image as from a Lord who is Spirit? Dr. Dale found it to be true, and the permanent value of his later works lies in their constant and triumphant appeal to religious experience, not the experience of the individual, but the experience of the commonalty of those who have received the Christian redemption, who, living the Divine life, are in contact with the presence and power of the Spirit of God. During his ministry he had borne the brunt of the controversies which commenced with Colenso and 'Ecce Homo,' and which ended at last in the breaking down of all authority which is permanently external. He saw what was coming, and he steadily endeavoured to place Christianity beyond the reach of all such assaults, to show that the Christian religion cannot be judged from any standpoint but its own, and that all true theology must in the end be the interpretation of the truths revealed in the experience of believers living and departed. He was thus able to vindicate finally the New Testament as itself the experimental and standard interpretation of Christianity. There are points on which we have ventured to differ from him, but on the whole there are no contributions to Christian theology made in our time so likely to endure as the series of volumes which includes *The Living Christ and the Four Gospels,* and *Christian Doctrine.* It is significant that these works seem to open up a new audience to Dr. Dale, and it was gladdening in the highest sense for him to know that he was fortifying the faith of the Church in his last days, as even he had never been able to do before. In intellectual power, in beautiful and stately expression, in wise, catholic interpretation, his last books are his best. However much we may wish that he had remained a little longer to give us the ripe fruit of his long meditation in his work on the 'Holy Spirit,' it is surely matter for joy and thanksgiving that he has given us so much, that he went on from strength to strength, and knew no waning and no decay in his intellectual and spiritual power. Of too many theologians what was said of the younger

Pitt is true—'He never grew, he was cast.' The diligent readers of Dr. Dale—and happily they are many—know that this is the last thing that could justly be said of him.

We leave to others better qualified to tell how sweetly and nobly his faith was manifested in daily life. It is impossible for us not to testify how many kindnesses we received from him, how many words of encouragement he wrote us, how considerate and steadfast was his friendship. From time to time, in spite of his weakness and his exhausting labours, he sent us contributions to these columns. These kindnesses, which meant so much to him who received them, were such matters of course in that beneficent career that he scarcely seemed to remember them. But there are hundreds all over the country who owe him what they cannot express, what they can never forget. God has been good to our Nonconformist churches in these latter days, and has given them many wise, gracious, and spiritual leaders, but none of them all has done a greater and more enduring work than 'our high Star and true Apostle that is gone.'

March 21, 1895.

A SPIRITUAL TRIUMPH: THE LIFE OF DR. JOHN CAIRNS[1]

THOSE who knew Dr. Cairns will be stupefied at the first sight of Dr. MacEwen's biography. It is a very stout and handsome volume of eight hundred pages. Dr. Cairns was so reticent, his life was so uneventful, his numerous letters were so brief, that it is difficult to imagine how such a book could be made up. But the biography is excellent, and fully justifies itself. There has been no Scottish ecclesiastical memoir of the same value published since Hanna's *Life of Chalmers*. It almost gives what is, after all, the incommunicable freshness of impression which comes from the contact with a living man. More than that, those who knew Dr. Cairns will find that this book helps to interpret him, and really adds to their understanding of his personality. While writing in the most affectionate and reverent spirit, Dr. MacEwen is rigorously truthful. We have here the story of a spiritual triumph, and something which came short of being an intellectual triumph. Dr. MacEwen throws a strong and faithful light on a deeply instructive history. That most serious and awful

[1] *Life and Letters of John Cairns, D.D., LL.D.* By A. R. MacEwen, D.D. (Hodder and Stoughton.)

description of Christian experience contained in the words, 'Ye died, and your life is hid with Christ in God,' rises to the mind habitually as these pages are read.

It must be acknowledged that Dr. Cairns started with great advantages. He was the son of Scottish Christian peasants, who bestowed upon him full health of body and mind. It may be doubted whether any lot could have been more fortunate, though the father and mother with their eight big children had for a time to content themselves with a single room, with bed recesses, and 'a milk closet six feet broad.' The indulgences and graces of existence were absent, but other things were absent also. There was no moral weakness weaving itself into life as an inseparable thread of darkness. There was a strong sense of law and duty, a Spartan simplicity, a serene and broad intelligence, a sober yet ever-pleasant and cheerful light of morning, a plain, undemonstrative fidelity, and, above all, a hallowing piety and faith. The fever of modern life, the tremors of sickly foresight and restless ambition, were unknown in this quiet world, where the generations went and came calmly. Dr. Cairns had, besides, throughout his life a singular immunity from sorrow. Not that he escaped the common lot—his affectionate nature was again and again sorely tried by the loss of dear friends and comrades. But his faith rose easily above such griefs in the assurance that, though clouds and darkness are round about God, yet in Him there is no darkness at all. He did not enter into the closest relationship of life. His biographer tells us that 'at the age of thirty-one he was the rejected suitor for a young lady's hand. At that time he was consoled by the hope of renewing his suit with more success, but presently she was married to another man. Stray notes in a holiday journal show that a fierce struggle followed, in which his whole nature was stirred, but he was victorious.' We read further on that he had thoughts of marriage up till about the age of forty, and then completely dismissed them. He was not a man to be tortured with unavailing broodings over what was left behind, and he was spared the passage through the heaviest clouds that can overcome humanity. Although this is not a point on which one can speak with confidence, it seems as if his heart never received a lasting wound. The supreme interest of religious biography often lies in the conflict of the soul succoured by grace with sin and grief. Such interest this biography does not possess.

On the other hand, it brings out with singular clearness the fine and strange combination of openness and reserve which is perhaps the ideal form of the Christian life. We should say about Dr. Cairns that nothing was more characteristic of him than his power of making himself at home with all classes of men. He might have represented St. Paul's words about being 'all things to all men.' Doubtless this was very largely a natural endowment, and indeed it must be this in part with every Christian. Dr. Cairns was enthusiastically human, full of the sympathies which are at the basis of human character. He was naturally drawn to men and women, aware of the richness of the common vital stock, sure about any stranger that if he knew him he would find much to love. If there is any natural gift that Christ takes under His protection it is this, and so Dr. Cairns found it. A universal good-will often loses itself fairly in sentiment, and is found incompatible with strong individual attachments, but Dr. Cairns's broad, out-reaching nature was always ruled by one purpose. He constantly longed and laboured to bring men under the power of that Love which had taken their burden to the Cross. This openness went along with a most curious reserve, which his biographer duly signalises. He did not seem to want companions. Through his wide-ranging journeys he travelled alone. Though very companionable and possessed of many devoted friends, he deliberately preferred to be solitary. During a pedestrian tour in the Lake District in 1849, he had a lofty and impressive religious experience, and the Borrowdale Hills were 'consecrated to him for ever by memories of God.' As Dr. MacEwen says, 'he found his Mount Hermon after happy days of eager sight-seeing and cheery talk with unknown foreigners.' It may be a complete error, but it seemed to the present writer that in his later days he even preferred the company of the poor and unlettered, and that he shrank from discussions of debated points in theology, choosing rather the freedom of that broad region where all believers are one.

Many will say that the chief thing notable, the first memory attached to his name, is that of his great and life-long humility. It is difficult, and would be impossible in our space, to give any idea of the extraordinary beginning of his career as a dissenting minister. On his University he left an unprecedented impression of scholarship and mental power. The highest hopes were cherished of his future, but his intellectual ambition died an early death. He was more than content with his lot as a Nonconformist minister in Berwick-on-Tweed, and it is not too much to say that, after a certain stage, he received everything which his Church brought to him in the name of religion with the tender faith of a child. He asked nothing from the Church, looked for nothing, desired nothing, except the satisfaction of labouring in what he believed to be the cause of God. But for that cause how great were his hopes, how manifold were his efforts! It was impossible to hide such a man, and when his head appeared above the level, it was inevitable that he should be called up higher. His career from beginning to end was full of pathetic refusals to accept the estimates and invitations of his fellow-men. Many of these he concealed. Dr. MacEwen tells us that in 1859 Dr. Cairns was offered the Principalship of Edinburgh University. He was then in his fortieth year, and his most exacting ambition might well have been satisfied, but he immediately declined the offer on the ground that he had consecrated himself to the service of Christ in the Church. But far more noteworthy and characteristic is the fact that he mentioned the offer to no one, and that his own brothers knew nothing of it until they examined his correspondence after his death. He had indeed died as few have died to worldly ambition, and he kept his secrets well. More than once we have come unexpectedly on traces of the good deeds he hid so jealously. No one ever knew how much of his time was spent in works of mercy and of prayer.

His Christian experience was, as might have been expected, singularly joyous and peaceful. He survived the failure of many hopes, but he was not ashamed. Dr. MacEwen tells us that the year which witnessed the breakdown of the Union negotiations between the United Presbyterian Church and the Free Church was perhaps the happiest of his life. To this cause he had given measureless labour and thought, yet the failure did not disturb him. It recalls Wordsworth's lines—

> 'From all doubt
> Or trepidation of the end of things,
> Far was I as the angels are from guilt.'

He took an active part in controversy from time to time, and made special efforts in the cause of Disestablishment. He acquitted himself bravely as a soldier in the uniform of Jesus Christ, and was indeed as true a crusader as ever took up the cross. But we do not know of his ever speaking a scornful or impatient word, nor do we remember that he was ever charged with insincerity, although exposed to misconstruction like others. The strong, simple, unselfish motive that impelled him was not to be mistaken. Yet in these discussions, while he plied his weapon well, there was about him a strange air of remoteness, as if his soul had soared beyond the field of battle, and looked down from the rest of victory. His zeal was wholly for the Kingdom of God, and he believed intensely that God was bringing that Kingdom through defeat and delay as well as through triumph. His life was above and beyond the incidents of the hour, and the secret of its tranquillity was that he was perfectly at peace with God, and found Christ made to him, moment by moment, wisdom, and righteousness, and sanctification, and redemption.

So his days ran on quietly, and men more and more deeply marked his goodness. When his health failed and his work had to be restricted, he was 'clothed as usual in unconscious cheerfulness. He talked frankly about his symptoms and his prospects as one who had no need to be troubled or perplexed.' His speech was free and hopeful, his spirit bright, his memory strong. Even when he had to resign, he wrote with the utmost calmness and cheerfulness, 'I am quite willing to take into consideration any hint for indoor work, if the outward be taken away. As to means of subsistence, I am thankful that I am so well in hand as to have no motive on that score to cling to anything. My mind is much relieved by the proceedings. God has been gracious, and my times, with those of all others, are in His hand.' How good it is to read such words! to see how, as the darkness closes in and the strength fails, there come the peace, the stillness, the dews of evening! He did not die beclouded by pessimism; he was not like the great Frenchman, Montalembert, with whom he had most curious intellectual affinities, and of whom it was said that a certain still despair lay at the bottom of his heart in the declining of his life. Dr. Cairns rejoiced in the unswerving hope of the glory of God, and as the splendour of the earthly sunshine was fading, he saw a new lustre rise.

To sum up: John Cairns was a living proof and illustration of the words of the Shorter Catechism, which was so dear to him: 'The benefits which in this life do accompany or flow from justification, adoption, and sanctification, are assurance of God's love, peace of conscience, joy in the Holy Ghost, increase of grace, and perseverance therein to the end.'

May 9, 1895.

PROFESSOR HENRY DRUMMOND

When we think of the friend we have lost, and of the prodigious influence he exercised over his fellow-men, it is his personality that always comes to the forefront. Born in a Christian home, ever under the influence of the most earnest and loving Christianity, he was himself not only naturally good, but naturally virtuous, to use the subtle French distinction. His tall, athletic form, his beautiful face, his rare union of strength and gentleness, of courage and tenderness, of boldness and sanity, gave him a charm which can be partly accounted for, but which in the end of the day we must call magnetic, for it could never be completely reduced to its grounds. He never showed that he had himself experienced the agonies and travails of religious conflict. But no man was more familiar with the battles and the defeats of his fellows. Humble and simple, always at the furthest remove from self-sufficiency, he was yet self-sufficing. The incalculable work he did as a father confessor of multitudes was apparently accomplished with triumphant ease. He was always willing to hear, to help, and to give, but he himself never asked anything, never seemed to need anything, and so far as one could see, had nothing to grieve over in the past, nothing to fear in the future, nothing to turn for to any friend save to his Saviour Christ. Though he well knew the sorrowful side of life, he himself never seemed till the last to be entangled in the coils of pain. His temperament was joyous, and he lived life with unfailing zest from sunrise to sunset. Such natures are so rare and separate that they cannot fail to be influential. Such a union of qualities, as Dr. Dods remarks, may not occur twice in a century. With the largest breath of sympathy, he yet held a faith which never seemed to be shaken or even clouded. In addition, he had very unusual endowments as an orator and as a writer. No one we have ever listened to impressed us quite in the same way. His words were the effortless utterance of a man with a message, a man who could clothe his thoughts in the simplest and at the same time the most shining vesture. Perhaps his main characteristic both as speaker and writer was his brilliant and untiring freshness. You might agree with him, or you might not, but you could not choose but hear and remember. As a stylist he occupied a high and singular position. What he wrote had the polish and the exquisite fitness of phrase which belong to a great literary artist. He was never turgid and never obscure. He had grasped with firmness the primal law that epithets must not be introduced for ornament, but only to give a real and pregnant meaning to the sentence. Of reporters he had a curious horror, a horror which is not easily justified, for he had so trained himself that his expression from the platform and from the press was equally consummate.

It followed naturally that his message was, before all things, gracious. Into whatever he spoke or wrote he put his own radiant personality. It is not our business to-day to discuss his theological system, if he had one; but to him, almost more than to any other preacher of the generation, the Gospel was good news, and he stood up to speak it as one fully inspired by its spirit. He did not endeavour so much to rouse or probe as to strengthen and soothe. It might be maintained with a great deal of plausibility that our Lord was wont at first to quiet the spirit of His hearers. He began with the beatitudes themselves, instead of insisting on the effort necessary to win them. At any rate, Drummond did justice to that restfulness of Christianity which lies behind its spiritual sharpness and searchingness. Many—and we count ourselves of the number—believed that he never had a complete intelligence of the religion of Redemption, simply because he had no adequate conception of sin, and no sufficient place for it in his teaching. But we have to remember both his own nature and the circumstances in which he appeared. When he began his public work in 1874, intelligent observers were declaring that the Free Church was hopelessly encased in an iron shroud of dogma, and that her days of influence were over. It was thought that the powerful and original men who founded the Church were to have no successors, that the very zeal of the Free Church had generated an impatience of independent thought that put it hopelessly out of harmony with the growing liberalism of the age. The Church, in short, was forgetting that this is the nineteenth century, and was undergoing a process of intellectual starvation. On the other hand, the Established Church was gaining command of mental power as fast as the Free Church was losing it. We do not think that any one would say so to-day, and the brilliant literary and theological renaissance of the Free Church is largely due to Drummond and to a few of his contemporaries. These men by no means abandoned, they have never abandoned their idealism. Drummond himself, with all his gentleness, his manliness, his shrewdness, never reduced revelation to the limits of sagacity. It would not be right to call him a mystic. No mystic could ever be so popular. It would perhaps be fair to say that he lacked the Hebrew and Christian perception of the veil veiling over all nations. But his was not one of those precise, definite, and narrow minds that rule off all possibilities at the visible horizon. It sometimes seemed in what he wrote or said that he fell into the dangerous argument that the most disinterested actions are in a sense interested, that if you could only lengthen out the vista of calculations far enough, you would find that virtue pays. But it was not so. He always acknowledged the higher will and the deeper purpose. In his nobler moods he was conscious of that mysterious world which wraps earth like an ocean of mist, and makes all horizons dim.

Many people were and are puzzled by Drummond's sympathy with Moody. They can understand very easily the immense debt, always acknowledged so proudly and generously, which he owed to Dr. Marcus Dods. But they cannot understand his occasional subordination to and constant sympathy with a man like Moody, who, for all his talent and even genius, cannot be said to be in the very least alive to the problems of modern Christianity. We do not think the difficulty beyond solution. Drummond was above all things practical. When he spoke he meant to achieve results, and he believed that they could be achieved at the very moment of his speaking. As the readers of *Natural Law in the Spiritual World* are aware, he maintained at first that there was a tremendous interval between the natural man and the spiritual man. He argued that the passage from the natural world to the spiritual world was hermetically sealed on the natural side, the spiritual world being guarded from the world next in order beneath it by a law of biogenesis. 'Except a man be born again he cannot see the kingdom of God.' It is not true to say that he held the natural man to be as remote from the life spiritual as a stone. But he did seem to maintain that the natural man is as remote from the life spiritual as a stone is from the life natural. Probably he would have shrunk in later days from such a comparison. He would not have insisted—perhaps he never would have insisted—that there must be a conscious turning to God at a fixed period of time on which you could lay your finger. But he did always believe, and he was right in believing, that if preachers aim at producing definite results, they can often do it. The great defect in most modern preaching is that it does not appeal directly and cogently to the will. Take the appeal at its lowest. Is it not true that many men have a latent feeling of unworthiness and hopelessness in their lives? They see that their course is not drifting to a fair end. It is often a great service if they can be made to feel that they need not travel as they are travelling, that they may reverse their course. 'I thought upon my ways, and turned my feet unto Thy testimonies.' Drummond had always a profound sense of the ruinous bent of innumerable lives, especially among young men, of whom he knew so much. He was aware of the countless wrecks due to sensuality. He feared, above all things, that paganism which smites the moral sense with decay. We remember his expressing himself vehemently on the vicious nature of a novel which, compared with much contemporary fiction, was comparatively innocuous. And so he spoke straight to his hearers. He appealed to their consciences and their reasons; he showed them that whether Christianity was true or not, they were taking the wrong road, and he constantly declared to them that they might form a friendship with Christ. A noble friend had an influence that changed into nobility, and if to live with men diluted to the millionth degree with the virtue of the Highest could exalt and purify the nature, what bounds could be set to the influence of Christ? Without a very strictly defined theology, he preached Christ as a potent influence whereby we can become what we are not through intimate communion with perfect love and perfect holiness. Thus he won his immense success with the most difficult classes—especially with students. They saw in him the likeness of Christ, and they gave him earnest heed.

> 'For to know good is to love it,
> And the honour that I covet
> Is the pride of your pure youth.'

Besides, with all the sense and sanity which could weigh the possible against the ideal, and strike the balance of wisdom between them, he had a profound sense of the incalculable sudden powers that work upon the soul. He knew that as he reasoned the involuntary rush of forces came up, often from half-hidden springs, that incredulity gave way not step by step as it was conquered by evidence, but with a revulsion of feeling, and passed at once into what might almost be called the opposite degree of conviction. No wonder that his speech often produced a magical instantaneous effect. But he left seeds in many minds which fructified in a way of which the world knew nothing. However his early theological dogmas might have changed, his addresses to the last might all have been delivered from the text, 'Turn ye, turn ye; why will ye die?'

We have only room for a few words on his apologetics and his theology. It is noticeable that he always seemed somehow to assume Christianity, never to argue for it. As we know that fire warms us, and that water quenches our thirst, so we may know that Christ has redeemed us. He believed that the evidences for the truth are both above and beneath the alleged evidences, and that Christianity can afford to stand speechless in the world's judgment hall, knowing that its works bear witness to it that it is of God. The present writer often urged upon him a work which he could have done incomparably well—a new Gesta Christi—an argument for Christianity from its effects. As to his theology, no theologian would admit that it was satisfactory or coherent. Of the Atonement, for example, he made nothing, not that he rejected it, but that he had no place for it, and received it as a mystery. Criticism did not in the least trouble him. He was not affected by any dogma on inspiration. Large parts of the Bible he was content to leave alone. At first he was Calvinistic, but always with a sense of the intention of Christ as Sovereign. He had no adequate conception of the idea of the Church as the place in which the scattered body of revealed truths which wander as pilgrims up and down through the world find a centre of unity and a definite home. We think he would have said that no reason can be given for that which lies at the basis of all reasoning, and that Christ was a living power before gospels were written, and would be a living power although they perished.

A word must be said about his eager and continued interest in science. To understand this, it must be remembered that his career began when Huxley and Tyndall were dominating the nation, and when it seemed that physical science was congealing into an intolerable universal despotism of material forces. He saw that the age was essentially scientific. He saw that there appeared to be between science and religion a spanless and fathomless abyss. He discerned that the materialists were swiftly poisoning the nation, and that they were following Comte in erecting materialism into a religious system. He threw himself with all his strength into the work of effecting a reconciliation, and though we do not propose in this place to discuss the value of his work, it may certainly be said at the very least that it helped to change the situation, and to bring into many minds, scientific and religious, more than a ray of hope.

In the noble and discerning tribute which Dr. Dods paid to his friend, he rightly signalised the fact that Drummond wisely and courageously chose his own course in life. He would not be the slave of conventionalities. He refused to run in grooves, or to undertake work that did not suit him. It is best for most of us that we should be compelled to do our work, but there are bright spirits who accomplish their best if they are left untrammelled, and he was eminently one of them. His friends were chosen from all classes of society. He had endless sources of pleasure. But he gave you always the sense that he was disengaged from them, that he was not dependent, that all might go, and that he would remain the same. And so these testing, terrible last years proved it to be—proved that his faith, his gaiety, his courage were no gifts of fortune and circumstances, but gifts of God that are without repentance. What can we say about the early close of his labours? Like so many others—Elmslie, Robertson Smith, Robert Barbour, Mackay of Uganda, belonging to the same Church, he has passed away in his prime. It may be that the best of his original work was accomplished, but there is little comfort in such thoughts. If he had lived he could have done what no man left behind him can do, and Drummond in good health would always have been a force of the first rank. We must take refuge in faith. We cannot see, but we may trust. It is something to remember that the exuberant and beneficent vitality in which we rejoice is not lost—not lost for us or for any who share the good hope through grace. Henry Drummond's departure for the new country has made the other life for many, in an unspeakable degree, more real and more winsome.

March 18, 1897.

REVIVAL CHRISTIANITY: PRINCIPAL BROWN[1]

Dr. Blaikie has been signally successful in his delineation of the late Principal Brown. This is one of the best religious biographies written for a long time, sympathetic yet discriminating; not too long, and yet not too bald; well arranged and full of interesting matter. Dr. Blaikie hits the white when he says that Principal Brown was naturally humble and contented. Many who did not know him well, and some who did, were of a different opinion. But we have no doubt that Dr. Blaikie is correct. A certain want of ambition and concentration made him miss distinctions and fail of achievements easily possible to him; and had it not been for his prolonged lease of health and life this loss would have been more conspicuous. We doubt, however, whether many of his contemporaries saw as many good days as the Principal. His happy disposition, his universal curiosity, his ready address, and his quick methods, his scattered but constant industry made his life fresh almost to the last. Every new day was a day of hope for

[1] *Dr. David Brown, D.D., LL.D.* By W. G. Blaikie, D.D., LL.D. (Hodder and Stoughton.)

him, and when it grew clear that the days on earth were numbered he hoped mightily in the day to come. Dr. Brown had very little success as an ecclesiastic. He had none of the qualifications which, according to a friend of ours (whom on this point we do not entirely trust), are necessary for ecclesiastical ascendency. He had not the art of clearing his throat in a lengthened and impressive manner—an accomplishment which, if our friend is to be believed, must be put in the very forefront. He could not speak slowly and deliberately. He was not a man of what is called a fine presence. He did not know how to use large gold eye-glasses, moving them up and down solemnly to the march of his speech, and laying them to rest where his delighted hearers might gaze upon them. He was not a master of such sonorous phrases as 'I desire to associate myself.' He could not pronounce the word moderator as it ought to be pronounced, that is as a word of at least twenty syllables uttered with infinite relish and with a lingering pride. He could not suppress his own personality, his own quickness, his own cleverness. To be a great ecclesiastic—we are giving our friend's view—an able man must rigidly suppress his ability, and a humorous man his humour, and a sarcastic man his sarcasm. Principal Brown could not suppress anything. He was as open as the day. In five minutes you could understand him.

Nor was the Principal a very successful professor. He was not a failure, and in some ways he did well, but he was not of the class of men who have great and abiding influences on students. After many years' study of the subject we frankly confess that we cannot tell what makes a good professor. Dr. Brown used to tell with much satisfaction that an old minister once said, 'I am not afraid to preach to probationers; I am not afraid to preach to ministers, but there is a thing called a divinity student. God preserve me from preaching to it!' 'There is a thing called a divinity student,' and that thing is a mystery. Some men, you might think, would most certainly win his worship, and yet somehow they do not. There is no failure in earnestness, in ability, in labour, in temper, it may be even in genius, and yet somehow the effect is missed. Others there are, and we have known them, who seemed to have everything against them, who are never by any chance conciliatory, who make no sacrifice to the graces, who are somewhat scornful of modern culture, and yet their students idolise them. All that can be said is that you can generally tell whether a man will be a successful professor by appointing him to a chair and hearing what the students say about him at the end of two years. This does not seem satisfactory, but it is all the length we have got. Principal Brown did not make his service what it might have been because he did not always do his best. It is unreasonable to ask that a man should always be at his best. That is, of course, impossible. But a man may always do his best, and he always should. He may be depressed, ill, weary, hopeless, burdened; but the work, whatever it is, must be carried through with as much conquest of circumstances as possible. There rise before our mind some whom we have known intimately, of whom you could always say this, that be their work or subject what it might you were positively certain it was the utmost they could do at the time, that if they failed they never failed for lack of effort, self-sacrifice, resolution. Principal Brown, when he girded his loins and thought and studied and wrote carefully, could do better than most, but often he was content to talk, and talking was much too easy for him, and the lapse into anecdotage too swift and deep. Nevertheless, as the years went on, and as it seemed as if he would 'dander about till the resurrection,' you rarely met him but he opened a grave of memories, and you were spellbound by the rising ghosts.

Principal Brown was certainly one of the most brilliant men we have ever known. He had many amiable and noble qualities—qualities of courage, of cheerfulness, of resilience, which appear more rare, more estimable, as experience of life increases. But what impressed us at first in him, and all through, was that he had a true zeal for souls. From the beginning to the end he was never so happy, never so much at home, as at a revival meeting. You saw the true man then as he joined in some passionate hymn of redemption, with the tears running down his cheeks, or listened tremulously, eagerly, and 'with such believing eyes' to an evangelist preaching on 'that most blessed thief who stole the Kingdom of Heaven,' or on the cry of the Spirit and the Bride. His conception of Christianity was that of a revival Christianity, and this conception dominated his life. It is worth thinking a moment of what this implies. It means in the first place that Dr. Brown found his true rest and home in the central truths of Christianity, the truths of regeneration and redemption. There is a Christianity much in favour now. It contains what Vinet called a portion and emanation of the truth, and consequently some of the promise of the life that now is, but which does not save or renew. There is an element in Christianity which can be made intelligible and congenial to the unrenewed nature. Much indeed has been recognised by the unrenewed nature, and even yielded to; that is, there are maxims of Christianity which have created a new civilisation. There is an honest admiration for the character of Christ on the part of many who do not own Him as Redeemer. It is possible that this kind of Christianity, this Christianity of secondary ideas and applications, may go on prosperously from year to year like a well-managed business. It may even go so far that the world may become Christian in a certain sense, but Dr. Brown would have held that such a victory was no real triumph of Christ. He would have fallen back on his revival hymns :—

> 'He suffered the just for the unjust,
> That the unjust might not die.
> *For these things were done in the green tree*
> *That they might not be done in the dry.*
>
> 'Oh! think of the love and the pardon,
> And ask, "Why should I die?"
> *For these things were done in the green tree*
> *That they might not be done in the dry.*'

No, the fundamental truths of Christianity and the live faith of the Church can never be made clear and lovable to any but the spiritual man. To the natural man the mystery of redemption will always be more or less unintelligible, and more or less odious. And the Church can only live in the world by successive individual transferences from the natural to the spiritual kingdom. In other words, the Church is always dying, always being raised again.

That is why we speak of revival Christianity. For it is by revivals of religion that the Church of God makes its most visible advance. When all things seem becalmed, when no breath stirs the air, when the sea is like lead, and the sky is low and grey, when all worship seems to have ended but the worship of matter, then it is that the Spirit of God is poured upon the Church, then it is that the Christianity of the apostles and martyrs, not that of the philosophers and Liberals, keeps rising, as Vinet says, from the catacombs of oblivion, and appears young and fresh in the midst of the obsolete things of yesterday and the day before. If Christianity be as she is, eternally a stranger to the world, she is not in any sense established there. The world is increased by every being born into it, but the Church has no natural increase, only a supernatural. The Church lives by capture, by booty, by winning over from the world the citizens that make her number. Nor is it too much to say with a great thinker that she can hardly be said to live at all. Her life is a perpetual resurrection, and she is for ever issuing from the tomb. This was Dr. Brown's view of Christianity, and it was this that made him delight in revivals. He saw Christ with his own eyes leading captivity captive. He knew that this was not the work of nature, but the work of grace, and in consequence in an age when faith in the supernatural supports itself by a struggle, his never wavered, we believe, for a single instant. It is only by grasping this view of the Church as fighting and struggling and suffering for every inch of ground that we can learn how much we depend on God, and how surely God is to be trusted. This view of the Church as not an establishment but an encampment in the world does not lead to despondency. It leads to the blessedness that comes from a constant nearness to the Eternal. Dr. Brown's Christian life was eminently happy, buoyant, exuberant, in spite of much that seemed threatening in the signs of the times. It is too true to say of many old men that during their last years their fears exceed their hopes, and their outlook for the Church of God is gloomy. '*A facie malitiae collectus est justus*' (Isa. lvii. 1) is what we naturally think when they die. But Dr. Brown recalled rather the strange saying of Bunyan, that there will come a time when Antichrist will be matter of history, when the saints will speak of how he grew and spread, and how he was consumed by the breath of the Lord's mouth, and destroyed by the brightness of His coming. Dr. Brown was not afraid to die, and, what is better, he was not afraid to live. He was too near the source of hope and quickening to be dismayed, and sometimes he would speak as of those who sit in the heavenly places with Christ Jesus, who look down on the conflict as though it was already passed, and behold the fallen Satan.

June 2, 1898.

WAS BISHOP WALSHAM HOW A PERFECT CHRISTIAN?

WAS Bishop Walsham How a perfect Christian? Judging from his biography, we almost think he was. We have never risen from any Christian biography with a similar impression of its subject. Of course we have to remember the drifted traditions Ruskin warns us against, which throughout the whole of history cover the vaults of searching fire that must at last try every man's work what it is. And there is great reason to rejoice in the new concern with Gospel law, though without the Gospel Gospel law is but a weight to sink us. People generally assume that while there is much variance on points of Christian dogma, all Christians are at one on points of conduct. The truth is, we have much more to learn about conduct than about dogma. Our whole standard and conception of what the Christian life may be and ought to be is under imperative need of revision. For ourselves we frankly confess that many characters and many biographies interest and attract us far more than the character and biography of Bishop How. And yet if we take the record of his life and set it beside the New Testament, we seem to discern a new and wonderful harmony, a transcript of the Lord in the disciple, which is almost a unique thing in religious literature.

To begin with, Dr. How from the beginning of his labour was a signal example of diligence and content. He was for nearly thirty of his best years rector of a comparatively small country parish. Yet from morning service at eight o'clock, till he laid down his pen about midnight, every day was fully occupied, and when he took up larger responsibilities he could say that no man can do more than work his whole time. It was said of him by a friend, and everything bears it out, that he was perfectly and absolutely content to live and die in his little parish. This is monitory and suggestive. It may be doubted whether Christians have taken fully to heart the parable of the talents, whether they clearly realise that our talents may be and must be doubled wherever we are placed, and that in every sphere, no matter how humble, there is always the opportunity and the call for unrelaxed diligence. There are Christians who are amiable and slothful, of whom their friends say that they have great talents, which have never yet found full development; Christians who salve their consciences by always talking about some great work they mean to do before they die. So far as we have noticed, these people are looked upon affectionately, without any passion of moral reprobation. Yet surely there can be no sin greater than this, no guilt heavier or more damning than that of the unlit lamp and the ungirt loin.

The world has been taught that its one standard of action and the one thing worth living for is happiness, and one can see how this evil teaching has gradually affected the general mind. In the view of Christ, our first business in this world is to do the will of God, and the happiness that is to be coveted is not the happiness that we pursue, but the happiness that overtakes us as we faithfully fulfil our task. Quiet spheres seem to give excuse for large intervals of leisure, but the Christian has no right to any leisure beyond the necessary rest. How found that he had more than enough to do. He would not even waste a few odd minutes. He would go to his writing-table and add a few lines to the book he was engaged upon. He ruled his life, as life can only be ruled, by being most absolute and rigid in method. When he knew that a letter had to be written, he would go and address the envelope so that it might serve as a reminder. And all this work was done with the most unbroken and steady content. In one church, ministers are asked at their ordination whether they will 'faithfully, diligently, and cheerfully' do their work. It is in the cheerfulness that most of them fail.

How had his trials like every man. He says that the only people with whom he was very successful were old women, but he was patient with the strange vacillations of morning and night that come to every Christian toiler. However narrow any man's allotted space of dominion may be, it is enough—enough for all his time and for all his energy. There is a strange contrast between his biography and that of his friend Edward Thring. Thring, if ever any man was, was a faithful and diligent worker. He went on resolutely through all his difficulties, but he almost destroyed the tonic effect of his life by his eternal groaning, and grumbling, and complaining, and self-pity. No doubt his difficulties were exceptional, though largely self-made, but if any one thinks that there is a sphere where there are no difficulties he is mistaken.

Most striking, and as it seems to us most Christian, was his total lack of ambition in every form but one. He was ambitious, as St. Paul was ambitious, to be well pleasing unto Christ. In the worldly sense he seems to have had no ambition at all. The sin that most easily besets Christian workers is perhaps the desire for a larger sphere, and it is plausible to say that the longing is lawful. But as a great churchman said, the Church as Christ conceived it has no place for secular aspirations, and in its ideal form should have nothing to encourage them. What is called the patrimony of the Church is perhaps to Christ only the golden chains of the arch enemy. Christ has endowed His Church not with earthly wealth and honour, but with the Holy Ghost. The New Testament has no suggestion in any shape or form that the ministers of Christ are to look for a more settled maintenance than their Master. When prizes exist in churches—and they exist in all churches, but very specially in the Church of England—they excite passions which are entirely foreign to the temper of Christianity. Even noble men have their lives marred and their hearts turned to bitterness by frustrated desire for promotion. We spoke some time ago of the Indian reformer, Baboo Keshub Chunder Sen, and his saying that if the people of the East adopted Christianity they would bring out into the light truths that Westerns have left in the shade. One such truth is that believers should be as dead to the ambitions of the world and as little touched by them as little children are touched by cheques or titles. When Christianity has worked its perfect work and Christians become as little children again, this will be so, and if there is any desire it will be the desire to go lower rather than to mount higher. It was so, eminently, with Bishop How. When he was offered the See of Manchester, a place of much greater dignity than he occupied in London, he declined it without even mentioning the matter to his wife. His purpose was that nobody should know of it, but it leaked out somehow. He accepted his call to the bishopric of Wakefield with genuine pain and simply as a matter of duty. When he was an old man he was offered the great position of Durham, with an income of more than double what he then had. Here, too, he decided absolutely, and only with the greatest difficulty allowed the refusal to become public. 'I wish,' he wrote to his daughter, 'people would not speak in such exaggerated terms about so very simple and obvious a duty as that of refusing Durham.' We are by no means sure that it was a duty, but he was the best judge. So it was with him through life—no envy, no grudging, but an unfeigned and unforced delight in the success of others. These qualities were his to the very last. We are not quite sure that modern Christian writers are in harmony with the New Testament in making so much as they do of sacrifice. Certainly it is true that the constant oblation of sacrifice unites us to the pure offering on Calvary, and that those within the Temple understand as outsiders cannot the increase of happiness that follows. But is it not the highest type of sacrifice to struggle to do those things as a matter of course —to be unconscious, as it were, that any sacrifice has been made ?

Bishop How also shines in what is one of the most straining tests of Christian character, the manner in which personal injuries are treated. We may sin by resenting them, and we may sin by forgiving them. Last week we referred to the letter Dr. Temple wrote to How after coming to London. How understood that he had the charge of the East End, and was not a mere suffragan bishop at the command of Temple. Temple set him right in terms which may be characterised as brutally plain or plainly brutal. The manner of his action was as remote from Christianity as it is possible to conceive. Imagine how Dr. Temple's letter might have been dealt with, and would have been dealt with, by the ordinary Christian. Walsham How was so popular and so prized that he could have without difficulty raised a storm of popular indignation before which Temple would have had to quail. Instead of this, he did what Temple should have done—he went and talked over the matter. He schooled himself to believe that Temple might be right, and did not allow himself to say one angry or disparaging word, though he felt that his work in East London was done. There is, we say, an un-Christian manner of forgiving as well as an un-Christian manner of resenting. In fact, in certain circumstances there is no greater sin than the sin of forgiveness. There is a demure conceit which receives all criticisms, however just, pityingly. The man never imagines that he is ignorant and vain and blundering, that he has much to learn from criticism. No, he forgives it ! You cannot forgive in the true sense unless there is an offence, and criticism is often an offence, but a duty. There was one, and one only, who could say, Whosoever speaketh a word against Me, it shall be forgiven him. Walsham How seems to have considered carefully and humbly all criticisms made upon him, but he himself would not consent to enter into personal quarrels, and we ask whether this was not in the highest sense of the word Christian. We may also ask whether it is not very rare.

We are conscious of entering on more delicate and difficult ground when we come to speak of

Bishop How's behaviour under the greatest of life's bereavements. There is nothing more fascinating in modern religious writing than its note of melancholy. Who among us has not owned the spell? The books that we take continually from the shelf and ponder over and over are the books that strike this note. To read and think of the dusky strand of death inwoven in all love, seems to bring us to the heart of Christ by a nearer way than any other. Think of the part which Death plays in all the nobler literature of the world! And assuredly the moment of calamity is the half-light in which much becomes visible that is veiled by the full glare of prosperity. Yet we may doubt very much and we doubt increasingly, whether this is perfectly Christian. There is no melancholy, as moderns understand the word, in the New Testament. It is 'bright and sun-beshone.' It passes through earthquake and through heartquake with a firm tread. It always indicates joy as the note of the Christian life: a supernatural joy in the midst of distress and grievance. We are to sorrow for the dead, but not bitterly, and never hopelessly, for the law which prevails on their shroud and on their dust does not prevail on them or on our vision of them, and the years that seem to remove us from their side are in reality bringing us nearer. For, indeed, there is no hour of human existence that does not draw on to the perfect day. The Gospel has a place for grief, but it is not nearly so great a place as Christian literature and Christian teaching often try to make it. True love is to nerve us for bearing sorrow, to make us pure by pain, by the forgetting of self, and by that forgetting of the past which is not oblivion, but much rather the anticipation of the future. To read lacerating passages from Bishop How's journal on his great bereavement would no doubt be a greater luxury than just to be told that he went and did his work, that he recovered his cheerfulness, that he was happy in the innocent enjoyment of life. But we suspect that in all this, as in other things, he was very near the mind of Christ.

Once more, there is something very admonishing in the manner in which the old man faced death. He saw it coming long before, but said little. He made all the preparations he could, wrote the fullest and clearest directions to his children on every matter, and even such small things as instructions to his successor with respect to ventilators and other details. He continued in excellent spirits, enjoying everything, and went on preaching. He arranged a fishing holiday in Ireland, and had some good sport. He was glad in the scenes of the beautiful world he was soon to leave. He had none of the morbid feeling that these things were shadows soon to pass :—

'When shall these phantoms flicker away
  Like the smoke of the guns on the wind-swept hill,
Like the sounds and colours of yesterday,
  And the soul have rest and the air be still ?'

There was nothing of the craving :—

> 'O, Paradise! O, Paradise! who would not long for rest?'

He was in the strait, no doubt, which St. Paul of old was in. He was willing to depart and be with Christ, which is very far better, and yet willing to remain in the flesh as long as that was expedient for any. Again, we ask, is not this in the full sense Christian, the thankful acceptance of all the blessings of earth? All of them were lightly held, and though he said little, there lay, no doubt, on all that last year of waiting the foreglow of the coming Angel.

November 3, 1898.

PRINCIPAL CHARLES EDWARDS

'He was the wisest man I have known, a Socrates in Life and in Death. There was no one I loved and honoured more.'

THE words came into our mind when we heard of Principal Edwards's death. Greater things might be said of one for whom to live was Christ, in a quite peculiar way, and for whom, therefore, death was a gain. His passionate personal love for our Lord burned like a hidden flame at the heart of all his thought and speech and action. There can be no hopeless sorrow for one who has passed in his Master's company through the shattered gates of death.

It is not for us to attempt anything like a biography of our revered friend. We shall try, however, to give some impressions of an intercourse necessarily limited, but lengthened, and occasionally most intimate. The present writer cannot but remember with pride that Dr. Edwards was one of those who helped in the establishment of this journal, and was a contributor to its first number. Many articles from his brilliant pen are scattered through its pages, and his friendly interest was maintained to the very end. We shall always be thankful to remember that one of his last acts was to remind us of a promise to visit him in spring, a promise which had not been forgotten. Every one who had the friendship of Dr. Edwards must feel that such a friendship was in itself a very great distinction. Of all the men we have ever known he was in many ways the most remarkable, the most individual. Were we compelled to put our impression of him into one sentence we should say he is the only man known to us since Spurgeon died, who might have been the founder of a great sect. He had the rare combination of necessary qualities. Absolutely disinterested, completely delivered from worldly ambition, fired with an ardent and constant passion, a great orator, a great thinker, and a born administrator, he was a natural leader of men. On the other hand, the large catholicity of his nature, his peculiar aversion to prominence, and his intense and affectionate loyalty to the Church in which he was born, prescribed the course of his life and service.

Dr. Edwards's unfeigned faith dwelt in his ancestors. He was of the best blood of Wales. For his father, Dr. Lewis Edwards, a thinker of wide outlook, massive power, and indomitable industry, he had a peculiar and growing reverence. His last task was a pious commemoration of that father's work in Wales. Dr. Lewis Edwards had ambitions for his brilliant son, and it was natural that he should go to London and distinguish himself there. A more daring step was his enrolling himself as a student at the University of Oxford. The old tradition, handed down from the days of the first Methodists, that Howell Harris had fled from Oxford as Lot from Sodom, still survived in strength amid the Welsh Nonconformists. Added to this there was a horror of the Puseyites, and an equal aversion from Jowett and the Broad Churchmen. Nevertheless, in the face of much opposition the step was taken and never regretted. The young Welshman soon made his mark at Oxford. He lost nothing of his old fervour, and he gained much. Among the notable Oxford leaders who were interested in him from the first were Benjamin Jowett and Mark Pattison. For both of these he had the warmest regard, for Jowett even a veneration. And he would quote to the last the words from the translation of Plato: 'One of the wisest and just and best of all men I have ever known,' and apply them to his old master. It was characteristic of Dr. Edwards that when he published his great work, his commentary on First Corinthians, he dedicated it to his father and to Jowett. This did not mean that he had moved from his father's theological position to Jowett's. Dr. Edwards was not, in the technical sense, a Broad Churchman at all. He was a keen student of such writers as Maurice, though held in the main by the older and profounder theology. He came to believe, and believed steadily, that there was such a thing as much love without much faith; and in another way he thought that Christianity was much more a matter of the heart than of the intellect, and judging them by this standard he pronounced Jowett and Pattison true Christians. He read with much enjoyment the posthumous volume of Jowett's sermons, and, speaking of it, said that at heart Jowett was a very true Christian. The young Welshman was particularly grateful to Jowett for advising him to exercise his gifts in the Church of his birth, although surprised that his master knew so very little of Welsh Nonconformity. At Oxford he acquired his fine mastery of the classical languages, and took the highest honours, while in philosophy he continued eagerly to pursue his studies. Dr. Edwards was no doubt a true humanist. An ὀψιμαθής he studied his Plato with continued devotion, and yet I think the classical writers never really won his heart. He would never have sympathised with the German scholar who gave his life to the study of the manuscripts of Petronius. He said, very characteristically, that all the classical writers were more or less deficient in depth of feeling, and he was never satisfied till he came in contact with the fervent heat of the New Testament. What he did at Oxford was mainly to master the tools which he needed in his profound investigation of the mysteries of the Christian faith.

Dr. Edwards began the work of the pastorate and ended it in Liverpool. Short though his time was there, it was influential, and there survives a graphic account of his preaching, from the very competent and sympathetic pen of Sir Edward Russell. Soon, however, he was called to one of the most prominent places in Wales, to the Principalship of the University College at Aberystwyth. In the opinion of most people, the great work of his life was done there. He had to face a most arduous task. To secure the establishment of the College, to carry it through its first difficulties, to meet occasionally almost overwhelming obstacles which presented themselves, was work which taxed even the strength of his magnificent youth. We suspect that he was led to this labour partly from his passionate love for Wales, and partly from his zeal for education. His feeling for the Principality was like Burns's devotion to Scotland, when he spoke of the wish that to the end ' would strongly heave his breast.'

> ' That I, for puir auld Scotland's sake,
> Some usefu' plan or beuk might make,
> Or sing a sang at least.'

And his zeal for education was inborn. Most competent witnesses have borne their testimony to the enthusiasm and self-sacrifice which carried the effort to triumphant success. To the very last his whole energies were absorbed. He had to act as Professor of Greek, to conduct the government of the College, and to raise funds. Nothing could divert him from preaching and theology, and he went through the country on Sundays like a flame of fire, throwing himself on the warm heart of the Welsh people. He found, of course, that they responded eagerly, and though influential men were against him the people were true, and carried him to victory. We shall not easily forget our experiences of his life there. It seemed as if the bell never ceased to ring. He would come in and tell you how an anxious parent had called, how some visitor had asked assistance, how some little trouble had arisen that needed to be settled. And so it went on for hours and hours of the day, the Principal taking all with nearly unruffled calmness. It was not till the night wore on, and till silence had fallen upon the street, that you could enter into real communion with him. Then he opened up his heart. Or he would drive you far into the beautiful country round Aberystwyth, and there, among the pleasant fields, he would rest and talk freely. In the ordinary sense of the word, Principal Edwards was not a brilliant conversationalist. In a mixed company he had not much to say, though he was a courteous and intelligent listener. Often he would answer a tolerably long paragraph with three or four words. He was at his best when alone, and yet even then it was never quite an exchange in the usual sense. If, however, he saw that you really wished to know his thoughts he would open up amazingly, and then his talk was as lucid and as pregnant as any I have ever heard. He did not care for personalities. I never knew him say an unkind word of a student or a minister. Some he would praise warmly, others less warmly, and of others he would say nothing, and thus you might draw your inferences. For his own people, and especially for his brethren, he had the warmest regard, and he would often deplore that Welsh thinkers like the late David Charles Davies and his colleague, Ellis Edwards, were so little known in England. But he loved to talk about the great themes of theology, about the interpretation of texts, about great dead divines, and sometimes, though rarely, he would speak of his own deeper experiences. Even when he said very little, what he said was always worth hearing and remembering. In a short sentence he could give a serviceable direction. There was no mistaking the constant current of his thought. It was always to the great revelation of God in Christ.

And now I shall venture to say what perhaps I have no right to say, what perhaps may be justly contradicted by those who know better. It appeared to me that great as was Dr. Edwards's influence at Aberystwyth, great as was the work which he accomplished, great as was his satisfaction at its success, he undertook and carried it through as an act of self-sacrifice. It diverted him much from the real object and delight of his life—preaching and the study of theology. But he was one of those for whom the mystery of life had been unlocked by the mystery of Christ's sacrifice, and so I believe that this was the sacrifice which he laid quietly upon the altar. Dr. Edwards always maintained a modest dignity. His ways were those of the scholar, of the Welsh gentleman, but his generosity was lavish, secret, and untiring. In speaking of his self-sacrifice one feels that there is a danger of being misapprehended. It was no sacrifice to him to give in the sense of suffering. It was his joy and delight. We remember a long discussion with him over Maurice's book on the Doctrine of Sacrifice, in which he strongly maintained that self-sacrifice was a law, even although no good might seem to come out of it. On his own consecration, on his countless acts of kindness, his lips were closed. He had such a great faith in the wisdom of ordaining love that I am sure he never doubted the guidance of his life. And yet some think that, if the time given to Aberystwyth had been devoted to theological work and study, Wales might have boasted of the most influential among nineteenth-century theologians.

At Aberystwyth, amidst all his varied work, he made time for his favourite theme. It was there that he wrote the classical Commentary on First Corinthians, which made him known to the world of letters and the Christian Church. The merits of the book have been recognised by such men as Ellicott, Godet, and Marcus Dods. It is much more than a commentary. It expounds as no other book does the doctrine of the Mystical Union. No one can read it thoughtfully, and remain quite the same. Much of it furnished material for sermons. Principal Edwards was thoroughly convinced that preaching came before everything else, and he believed that preaching would never have its due unless it dealt with the profoundest mysteries of the Christian faith. One memorable sentence he used more than once—' A great preacher is Christ's last resource.' He meant that when faith was decaying, when the Church was cooling, the hope was in the sudden appearance of a great preacher. Preaching, he said, would continue in the Church to the ages of ages, for Christ would not leave His people to die. We had a bond of union in our common admiration for the preaching of Mr. Spurgeon. Dr. Edwards seemed almost to struggle for words in trying to express his sense of Mr. Spurgeon's transcendent genius. What he specially admired in the preacher of the Tabernacle was that he could expound Christian thoughts in their depth and richness in adequate language, and apparently without a struggle. The masterful repose with which Mr. Spurgeon took hold of texts, which almost seemed to say the unsayable, and revelled in preaching them to the common people, constantly moved Dr. Edwards's wonder. The mystic knows the mystic; the theologian knows the theologian. A great mystic and a great theologian, Dr. Edwards knew that in Mr. Spurgeon he was in the presence of a teacher even deeper than himself, though his own scholarship was so far superior. No one who ever heard Dr. Edwards preach will forget the experience. He began with his little Bible in his hand, speaking slowly in a low voice, and gradually rose to the height of eloquence and passion. He never lowered his preaching, but, like Mr. Spurgeon, brought his hearers face to face with the most august themes.

I

When Spurgeon, as a youth, came to London, he did not preach about the anecdotes of the Bible, but took for texts: 'Accepted in the beloved,' 'No man can come unto Me except the Father which hath sent Me draw him,' and so plunged into the deep sea. In the same way Dr. Edwards from the first asked his hearers to think, and to think profoundly; but his thoughts were all of them fused in passion.

At last he had his way, and went to be Principal at Bala—too late, and yet not too late. There he was most generously supported by his Church. His hands were upheld by sympathetic colleagues, and he had great happiness among his students. Dr. Edwards had plans for literary work. He was to gather together the fruits of his long labour. He hoped, in particular, to give the final results of his study of the Epistle to the Hebrews. There was something in that book which always attracted him. Its calm passion, the peculiar depth and subtlety of its thought, its miraculous penetration into the heart of the Old Testament, and its many difficulties, drew Dr. Edwards by an irresistible spell. Some of his favourite sermons were taken from texts in the book, but, as he said to us, he never felt that he understood it as a whole. He would say that he fed on the bits of herbage that grew on the crags. But the mystery remained a mystery. He published, however, admirable essays towards its interpretation in his *Expositor's Bible* volume, and in a Welsh book for Bible classes.

He had great hopes of being able to give his final conclusions in the International Critical Commentary, but was obliged to abandon the work. Whoever the author to the Epistle to the Hebrews was, he must have been a kindred spirit to Dr. Edwards, 'an eloquent man, and mighty in the Scriptures,' and a subtle, devout thinker. Dr. Edwards loved to talk of the author's doctrine of the Atonement as it bore upon God, Satan, and the children, and his argument for the Sabbath-keeping to which the people of God attain, moving from rest to rest, and of many other thoughts the Epistle stirs. Alas! it was very soon clear that his strength was sapped, and that he could not do very much more. He could do much, no doubt. His lectures were eagerly appreciated, and his name was a tower of strength. His counsels grew more weighty, and his friendships warmer, and yet the dreams of youth and middle age were not to be fulfilled. Then there was a revelation more beautiful than any that even he could have put in profound writing or eloquent speech, of Christ's work in his soul. He enjoyed—and the fact was visible—a singular rest in God. He had lost his life and found it again, according to the word of the Lord. His love, his humility, his resignation, and even his joy, touched those who met him with a kind of awe. There were no repinings and no regrets. In his own humble way he felt that he had finished the work God had given him to do, and looked forward. Watchers were reminded of Pater's fine words:

'The infinite future had invaded this life perceptibly to the senses, like an ocean felt far inland up a tidal river.' He was recollected, loving, and calm. We have been deeply moved by Professor Ellis Edwards's account of his contempt of death. There was about Dr. Edwards most noticeably that 'solemn scorn of ills,' which seals the great saint. He was very sensitive, very modest, easily wounded, yet with a certain high disdain of life's dangers and evils. We cannot but recall the fine words of Amesius, a theologian whom Dr. Edwards warmly appreciated :—

> 'Concerning death, the first question is whether it be a thing to be contemned. Comparison being made betwixt death and these things which after death are prepared for the faithful, death may and ought in some sort to be contemned by all believers.'

How should we grudge our dear friend his rest? He was ever a student of divinity, and all that has happened is that he has gone to study where the divinity is clearer. And so many fellow-students, so many venerated teachers, have gone before :—

> 'Good-night, and not good-bye,
> Good-night, and best good-morrow when we wake.
> Yet why so quickly tire? Well we must make
> Haste to be done and die.'

March 29, 1900.

BISHOP WESTCOTT

The Bishop of Durham, who was taken ill after his farewell address to the miners in Durham Cathedral on Saturday week, died on Saturday night, surrounded by his family, conscious and cheerful to the last. In May he lost the beloved wife to whom he had been united for nearly fifty years. Doubtless the blow brought the close nearer, but he retained his courage, his cheerfulness, his undaunted optimism till his long labour ended in the home which he so dearly loved. Few sunsets have been more splendid. Nearly all the greater plans of his life have been accomplished to the satisfaction of his own exacting conscience. Happily he was spared, like Browning, to see his last book, *Lessons from Work*, a book of special value in these disheartened times. It has a tonic quality. It contains little that will be new to his students, but it strikes, as even he seldom struck, the ringing notes of high faith and hope. He lived and worked and died in the certainty of the Christian faith. The truth of truths never broke away from him.

Westcott will always be remembered as one of the great Cambridge triumvirate, the other members being Lightfoot and Hort. It is as impossible to dissociate his life and work from theirs as to dissociate theirs from his. The late Archbishop Benson was a close friend through life, and a fellow townsman, but his activities were mainly ecclesiastical, and intellectually, in spite of all his gifts, he was not on the same level. It is important to note that both Lightfoot and Hort were Westcott's pupils. Lightfoot spoke of him at the outset with the warmest admiration as 'one of the most gentlemanly, quietest, humblest, and most conscientious of mankind, to say nothing of cleverness.' This was in March 1848, and it was in 1849 that he became private coach to Hort, on whom his influence was no less great. Born in Birmingham in 1825, the son of F. B. Westcott, secretary of the Botanical Gardens, Westcott went to King Edward Sixth Grammar School, and there fell under the powerful influence of Prince Lee, whom he always considered one of the greatest teachers of his time. The *Times* is wrong in saying that he made friends there with Benson. Though Benson was at the school, the two men did not become acquainted till Benson went to Cambridge. When Westcott passed from Birmingham to Trinity College he had a very brilliant career in a very brilliant time. He graduated in 1848 as twenty-third wrangler, and was bracketed Senior Classic with C. B. Scott, afterwards headmaster of Westminster School. Professor J. E. B. Mayor came next, and amongst those in the first class were Mr. Llewelyn Davies and Bishop Barry. A Fellowship at Trinity followed, and shortly after he was ordained by Prince Lee, at Manchester. In those days his interests were very various, and nearly all of them told on his future work. Thus he was fond of music, and along with Henry Bradshaw and others was a member of the Choral Society. It is said by those competent to judge that not the least admirable of his publications is his *Paragraph Psalter*, an edition of the Psalms appointed for use in Peterborough Cathedral. The book shows the advantage of some knowledge of music as part of a clerical education, and recalls the days when the precentor of a cathedral was almost the highest in rank of its members. He anticipated the Psychical Research Society by founding a 'Ghostly Guild' for the investigation of apparitions. The members were disposed to believe that such things really existed, and determined to find out the truth. Westcott drew out a schedule of questions, and most of his friends joined him, but little came of the scheme. He was also, like Hort, interested in the Christian Social Movement led by Maurice, Kingsley, and Ludlow, a movement which, though seemingly abortive, has come to much and very much, which will come to more. We do not gather that he went so far as Hort, who was a contributor to the *Christian Socialist*, but seeds were sown in his mind which resulted in fruitful harvest. His first book was the Norrisian Prize Essay, issued in 1851, under the title of *Elements of the Gospel Harmony*, and extended nine years afterwards into the well-known *Introduction to the Study of the Gospels.* It is now in its eighth edition, and was an extraordinary achievement as coming from a young man of five-and-twenty. It did not miss almost immediate recognition. Hort, who perhaps was always inclined to concede more to criticism than either Westcott or Lightfoot, said that the discussion of inspiration was 'a wonderful step in advance of common orthodox heresy,' and wrote a review of it in the *Guardian.* The late Dr. John Cairns, who was then writing on German Theology in the *North British Review,* referred to the book in terms of high praise as a proof that it is possible 'to be a debtor to Germany without being a slave, and to contend intelligently, thoughtfully, yet charitably, for the doctrine of inspiration.' Westcott gratefully recognised the kindness of his unknown reviewer, and Mr. Macmillan tried to bring the two men together, an attempt defeated, we may surmise, by Dr. Cairns's invincible modesty. But the exact scholarship, the wide range of reading and the penetrating quality of thought in the book pointed out Westcott's true line in life, and this was not broken when in 1852 he accepted a temporary appointment at Harrow in place of a master named Keary, who died. Dr. Vaughan was at the head of the school, and offered the vacant position to Westcott, who accepted it with the full purpose of continuing his work on the New Testament. On a memorable day in 1853, during a visit to Birmingham, where Westcott met Hort, the two agreed to edit a Greek text of the New Testament. Westcott's work as a teacher during his seventeen years at Harrow did not count for very much in his life. He did not care for games, and the subtleties of his scholarship were lost upon ordinary boys. One of his pupils says: 'I remember that he took two whole Sunday lessons in discovering a "great verse in Galatians," and when the verse was set in examination at the end of term, two boys could not even translate it.' His influence, however, in other ways than the direct communication of knowledge was very valuable, and his biographer will no doubt take account of the *Public Schools Report*, published in 1874, where Westcott's examination is given. From this we make a curiously interesting quotation, as it seems to have been overlooked in all the newspapers:—

'1189. (*Lord Clarendon*).—You consider you stand [to the boys in his house] entirely *in loco parentis*?—Absolutely. The idea of a small house is that of a family. 1190. You think, then, that you would be able to put yourself in the place of a parent more effectually than any of the masters of the large houses who are *de facto* private tutors to their boarders?—It could hardly be otherwise. My boys would feel less scruple in consulting me, and they have free access to me at all times.'

He retained his mastership till 1869, serving most of the time under Dr. Montagu Butler. In 1885 he issued his *General Survey of the History of the Canon of the New Testament*, which shows even in a more marked form all the merits of his first book. It was characteristic of him to bring his new editions up to date, but just as the *Introduction to the Study of the Gospels* maintains the original thesis of *Elements of Gospel Harmony*, contending that, though the Gospels are not adequate materials for a biography in chronological order, they yet are not only adequate for their actual purpose as a revelation, but are trustworthy, though incomplete, as historical documents and complete as a Gospel, so it is with the second book. In the edition of 1875 he replied to the strictures of Mr. Walter R. Cassels, the author of *Supernatural Religion*. Mr. Cassels had rashly attacked Westcott, and had moved the wrath of Bishop Lightfoot, who fiercely resented imputations on his friend's scholarship and good faith. Westcott replied in a crushing but perfectly courteous way—in fact, with the calmness of a composition master. He could not conceal his amazement at the extraordinary blundering of his opponent, but he was much more respectful than Lightfoot and Salmon. The book was partly abridged and partly expanded as *The Bible in the Church*, and its scope was extended to take in the history of the Old Testament Canon as well as of the New. So far as the New Testament Canon is concerned the book is, as Hort says, 'as thoughtful, solid, and thorough a piece of work as you will not often see.' Meantime he was busy with other schemes. He kept on working with Hort at the text of the

Greek Testament, and would go from Harrow to Hort's country parsonage near Hitchin during his vacations, and toil for several hours a day. Hort and Lightfoot came really to know one another about 1856. Hort pronounced Lightfoot 'Westcott's best pupil. He always seemed solid, a great scholar, and disposed to be a learned and thoughtful theologian, but I was hardly prepared for the vivacity and liberality which he has shown in the last few months.' The friends laid out a scheme for a commentary on the New Testament. It makes one's mouth water to read it. To Westcott were assigned St. John's Epistles and the Apocalypse, to Hort the Synoptic Gospels, the Acts, James, Peter, and Jude. Commentaries by Hort on the Synoptic Gospels and the Acts would be simply priceless in these days, but Hort could not bring his thoughts to the birth as the others could. Westcott did not write on the Apocalypse, but he took Hebrews, which was originally assigned to Lightfoot. Hort was partly deterred by thinking that his colleagues insisted on the absolute infallibility of the New Testament. While he believed that it was possible there might be no errors, yet he thought it hardly probable, and he insisted on *a posteriori* criticism. He was disabused of his fears, but never had strength or heart to face the allotted task. Another project was a reply to *Essays and Reviews*. The triumvirate viewed with little satisfaction the attitude of the so-called orthodox party, agreeing in this with Dean Church, and they thought much of the clamour unfounded and unjust. Westcott himself warmly defended Temple against the attempt to remove him from the head-mastership of Rugby because he had contributed to *Essays and Reviews.* But the friends thought the book superficial, and they planned to give a reasoned and scientific defence of historical Christianity. This time it was Lightfoot who broke down. He found that he could not do his part, his burdens being already more than he could carry. Westcott afterwards published in 1866 a volume on *The Gospel of the Resurrection*, which has affected theological thought as much as anything he ever wrote. In an interesting letter to the late Dr. Reynolds he said that his own personal experience of the modern sceptical school in England was almost entirely confined to young University men, and their objections had been in his mind while he was pondering over the arguments which he had now tried to express through many years. In this letter he defended his obscurity. He considered it better to suggest than to develop thought. 'An adversary or a waverer may be won by an argument which is, he feels, his own, when he would be inclined to question it if it were placed, I believe, before him.' The *History of the English Bible* was also written during his Harrow days, and admirable as it is, it is perhaps not on his own level; in fact, it has been pronounced 'the least interesting and the most disappointing of the author's works.' It is at present out of print, but we believe a new and thoroughly revised edition will be published soon, and that Dr. Aldis Wright has taken part in the revision.

All this time promotion had tarried, but in 1868 Magee, the Bishop of Peterborough, made him Examining Chaplain, and in 1869 promoted him to a residentiary canonry in the cathedral, with an income of £540 and a house. The change was welcome, for his health was breaking down under his work at Harrow. He set himself immediately to promote theological learning in the diocese, and his preaching, which was greatly admired by Maurice, was most acceptable, though it had nothing of the popular power of Magee. In 1870 he was appointed to the Regius Professorship of Divinity at Cambridge. Here he found his legitimate place and true sphere of work. We have been told that his promotion was due to the great generosity of his friend Lightfoot, who might well have had the place, but was content to hold the Hulsean Professorship. It was a great time for Cambridge when Hort joined these two, and when the incomparable trio were members of its theological staff. Maurice, then nearing the end, was also very happy in Westcott's appointment, and felt that he had at last a coadjutor whose ears were open. About this time Westcott eagerly took up the plan for the revision of the New Testament. He did not quite approve of all the details of the scheme, but thought it very much better than might have been expected. In his quiet way he was always a leader, and it was he who suggested the Communion Service which began the work, a service which led to much controversy. In this year 1870 the Westcott-Hort edition of the Greek New Testament was in the press, but it was not published till 1881, and might never have been published had it not been that the Revised Version was to come out. It was thought desirable to anticipate the Revised Version, and the feat was accomplished with just five days to spare. Probably no work has ever been so long in going through the press, but the result justified the labour, and the Westcott-Hort text practically holds the field, and will hold it till scholars of equal rank after the same toil produce their results. Even more important were his great commentaries on St. John, the Epistles of St. John, and the Epistle to the Hebrews. Some of his works, including *Christus Consummator* and *Lessons of the Revised Version of the New Testament* were first published in the *Expositor*. There was no more kind, courteous, and obliging contributor than Dr. Westcott. In the Revision Committee the influence of Westcott and Hort was dominant.

In 1879, Lightfoot went to Durham, and Westcott preached the sermon at his consecration—'perfectly unique in the fierce love of it, and the tremendous charge for bishops to choose between the important and the routine of their lives, and to do the important.' Later on, in 1890, when he was in his sixty-sixth year, he succeeded Lightfoot. 'I come,' he said, 'in simplest obedience, offering the little I have without reserve.' Lightfoot had been very successful at Durham, though some shook their heads at his attitude to the Salvation Army. Westcott found in the office a new spring of life. He was able to apply his long cherished principles, and he did so with singular effect, being instrumental in settling the great strike in 1892. He introduced the system of sending home-clergy into the mission field for a term of years, and sent four of his seven sons to do missionary work in India. But the work of a bishop, however important, becomes separated from his personality, and Westcott will live as one of the greatest of Biblical scholars and theologians.

We had hoped to consider at some length the peculiar qualities of his contribution to criticism and theology, but the limitations of space forbid. It must suffice to say that his main characteristic was his fine classical scholarship. In that the Cambridge Biblical school immensely surpassed their Oxford contemporaries. Lightfoot in an early essay handled Stanley and Jowett severely, and, as Dr. Sanday says, his conclusions have never been questioned. They also proceeded on a strictly scientific method. All of them, and especially Westcott and Lightfoot, were conservative. They yielded very little to modern criticism. When Westcott reviewed Sanday's book on John he praised it warmly so far as it went with his own conclusions, but expressed his dissent from Sanday's free handling of the discourses, and his confidence that further study would bring him to a sounder view. Westcott was a mystic as well as a scholar, but his mysticism was not suffered to take the place of science. No commentaries have been more valued by great Christian teachers than his. Dr. Maclaren of Manchester, we believe, puts them above all others. Dr. Dale in one of his most finished pieces reviewed with enthusiasm the commentary on St. John's Epistles. On the commentary on Hebrews opinions somewhat varied. In our columns Principal Edwards of Bala described it as 'a beautiful rather than a great commentary,' and Dr. A. B. Bruce endorsed this view. But we have heard Dr. Dale, whose own exposition of the Hebrews is a really valuable book, refer to it with almost rapturous admiration, and if we are not mistaken it was Dr. Fairbairn who wrote the warmly appreciative and yet thoroughly critical review of it which appeared in the *Speaker*. There can be no doubt that Westcott was in little sympathy with Pauline modes of thought, and in this he was followed by the late Professor Milligan. Dr. Dale considered that Westcott was of all men the most qualified to write a treatise on the Atonement, because the explanation of the Atonement was to be found in that mystical relation between Christ and humanity realised in the Church on which Westcott dwelt so long and constantly. Dale thought that though in life the objective had as a rule to be believed first, in theory it was reached last. Nevertheless Dale could see that Westcott did little justice to the objective aspects of our Lord's sacrifice, and he felt, as many readers have felt, the reluctance of Westcott to define his thought. Westcott's real attitude to theological systems is indicated in one most significant sentence in his essay on Origen: 'No fact, I think, is sadder in the history of religious thought than that Augustine had no real knowledge of Greek.'

With some leading Nonconformists Westcott's relations were close and cordial. They were particularly so with Dr. Dale, whose work on the Ephesians was one of his favourite books. Years ago we were permitted by Dr. Westcott to publish in the *Expositor* his own favourite photograph of himself. We ventured to consult him as to the choice of a contributor to supply the accompanying appreciation. Dr. Westcott expressed his wish that Dr. Dale should write the essay. Much as Dr. Dale wished to gratify his revered friend, the state of his health prevented him. Dr. Reynolds was another friend, and much more intimate was the late Dr. Moulton, who worked along with Westcott on the revised translation of the Apocrypha. But even Dr. Moulton could not induce Westcott to take part in the celebrations of the Centenary of John Wesley's death. Westcott believed in an external unity of the Church, though he regarded with the kindest feelings Christians who were still separated from himself. Among the preachers who most fascinated him was Edward Irving, and he showed extraordinary interest in the reminiscences of Irving which were published in the *Expositor* by the late Dr. David Brown. Among the writers to whom he loved to own his obligations were two from whom he differed profoundly, but from whom he learned much—Baur and Comte. We cannot better close this inadequate sketch than by quoting from Bishop Westcott's last book these noble words: 'Can we call an opinion or a practice "catholic" when it is opposed to the deliberate convictions of multitudes of believers not less fertile than we are in Christian works? In India, to take one example only, the non-episcopal bodies, as far as a conclusion can be drawn from the latest statistics to which I am able to refer, do apparently twice as much for missions as is done by our own Church and the churches in communion with it. We cannot dissemble the facts; we cannot summarily dismiss them.' We have spoken of Dr. Westcott's gifts and his noble and pure use of them. Behind these there was a character of grand simplicity, humble, winsome, real and tender, a character which inspired the unwearied hope and labour in which he lived and died.

August 1, 1901.

JAMES MARTINEAU[1]

Dr. James Drummond, of Oxford, has undertaken the purely biographical part of Dr. Martineau's life, and this occupies nearly one and a half of two volumes. The other part is an exposition by Professor C. B. Upton, formerly his colleague, of Dr. Martineau's philosophical work. Dr. Drummond's contribution will be received with entire respect and gratitude, but it is disappointing. The author is a scholar of high rank, and a man of noble candour. These qualities are known to all readers of his book, *Via, Veritas, Vita.* But he is notably deficient in the faculty of expression, and he has none of the biographer's special gift. The book adds very little to our knowledge of Martineau, and leaves his personal character as much an enigma as ever. The chances are constantly missed. For example, there is no attempt at picturing the Liverpool of Martineau's day. There are no side lights; there are no vivid reminiscences; there is nothing to show the effect of Martineau's ministry, which was, doubtless, very great. In the same manner, the London ministry is hardly described at all. It was a very wonderful ministry.

[1] *The Life and Letters of James Martineau.* By James Drummond and C. B. Upton. (Nisbet and Co.)

It brought together men of all types. The congregation at Little Portland Street Unitarian Chapel was singularly representative, but of all this Dr. Drummond has practically nothing to say. Neither does he set Martineau in the framework of his friendships. In some ways Martineau was singularly accessible, and if Dr. Drummond had tried to collect facts, he might have told us much of Martineau's associations alike with State Churchmen and Free Churchmen. We should have particularly liked to read about the friends Martineau made in Scotland, and their impressions of him. Neither are we told much of Martineau's home life. The one new fact here is that Mrs. Martineau, twenty years before her death, suffered more or less from mental affliction. Much might have been said about Russell Martineau, for some time his father's colleague, and for long well known to all frequenters of the British Museum. But on all this Dr. Drummond is silent, or reticent to the highest degree. Never was there a more shadowy figure than the man Martineau as he is presented in these volumes. The letters, too, have very little personality. Most of them are like pages from his books, very well expressed, of course, and very stately, for Martineau seems to have lived day and night in full dress, but strangely devoid of humanity. By far too much space is occupied in accounts of Martineau's sermons and addresses. All that might safely have been left to Mr. Upton. Of him it may be said that he has discharged his duty to admiration. He is a thoroughly competent metaphysician, and has a real mastery of Martineau's writings. We have not found any reference to the remarkable little book based on Martineau's lectures by Professor Henry Stephen of Calcutta. The criticism, however, we should be disposed to make is that the life should have occupied two volumes, and the exposition of the philosophy should have been thrown into a third. As it is, Dr. Drummond and Mr. Upton are largely engaged in the same task, and those who wish to know Martineau's life better will be disappointed. Neither of them, it should be said, enters with any thoroughness into Martineau's position as critic and theologian. It could not be expected that Dr. Drummond should sympathise in the extreme scepticism which was the last phase of Martineau's opinion.

We turn to say something of Martineau as a man, as a writer, as a philosopher, and as a preacher and theologian. In all these capacities there seems to have been about him a certain zone of chill. He doubtless had a fervent heart, but that heart was hard to reach. In the personal episodes of controversies recorded by Dr. Drummond there is an evident element of harshness. We refer specially to his two battles with his sister Harriet. The first of them turned upon her demand that her old letters should be burned. She was afraid that they might get into print. Her brother absolutely refused to surrender them. They were interesting records of the past to him, and he would rather preserve the past than sacrifice it to the future. So he calmly broke off the friendship. It seems to us that his conduct was impossible to defend. Miss Martineau was quite entitled to ask for her letters. The brother who would rather lose the living friendship of his sister than part with a collection of dead letters could have been no brother at heart. Neither is it easy to think that Martineau was right in the final controversy. Harriet Martineau joined with a Mr. Atkinson to write a foolish atheistical book, and her brother savagely criticised it in his review under the insulting title, *Mesmeric Atheism*. We have just read the review over again. As Dr. Drummond confesses, it does not bear out Martineau's own description of it. It is thoroughly bad in tone and temper. Whatever aberrations of judgment his sister might have been guilty of, it was not for her brother to expose them in that fashion. On the other hand, Martineau certainly had some warm friends, as well as many admirers. Among the closest was R. H. Hutton. We gather from this biography how bitter was the mortification which Hutton endured when he found that there was no place for him in the Unitarian ministry. On great questions of faith he separated himself from his old teacher, but the attachment between the two does not seem to have waned, and to Hutton's steady and strenuous championship in the *Spectator* Martineau owed much of his late fame. The controversy which took place over Manchester New College, when J. J. Tayler and Martineau were appointed professors, was not pleasant. We gather that Mr. Vance Smith was removed because he could not control the students. It was proposed to retain his services as teacher of Hebrew. To this Martineau offered the most determined opposition, and his own son received the appointment. This was not done at Martineau's instigation, but it was very agreeable to him. On the other hand, he behaved very well when Croom Robertson, then an unknown young man, was appointed over his head to the Chair of Philosophy in University College, London. It is painful to read that John Stuart Mill would not allow his testimony to Martineau's fitness to be used, as he could not miss the opportunity of planting a disciple of his own school in an influential position. Archbishop Thomson, of York, in reply to an application from Martineau, kept silent for a year, and then wrote that if he had helped he would have been assisting to a place of power one who did not believe in the doctrine of the Trinity. This is very painful, but Martineau bore no grudge, and afterwards became an intimate friend of Robertson's, who was a man of high ability and noble character. What is most admirable in Martineau's life is its lofty and serene dignity. 'A great soul in a small house' was the spectacle that fixed Lacordaire's admiration. If the great soul dwells contentedly, nobly, in the narrow surroundings, then he deserves reverence. As Hutton said, Martineau would have drawn thinkers from all parts of the world if he had lectured in any great university, but, as a matter of fact, he was engaged in discoursing to 'two or three boys in a corner.' What he did for these 'boys' is shown in the fact that the great books of his last years were mainly recasts and digests of the lectures he prepared for them. There is something very noble also in the patience with which Martineau worked without recognition. Up to his sixty-fifth year he attracted very little attention, though his essays were reprinted in America and his *Endeavours after the Christian Life* slowly won its way among religious readers. He was in his seventy-seventh year when his study of Spinoza was published. The *Types of Ethical Theory* appeared when he was eighty, and his *Study of Religion* when he was eighty-two. His academic eminence was recognised by Edinburgh shortly before his eightieth birthday, by Oxford when he was eighty-three, and by Dublin when he was eighty-seven. But Martineau worked always for higher ends than fame.

To many of us the greatest wonder about Martineau is his style. He had an unrivalled mastery of expression. He could turn out, apparently without effort, sentence after sentence, page after page, of subtle, strong, varied, precise, and stately English. Whatever he was writing—letters or sermons or philosophical treatises—he is always at the same high level. There seems no bound to the riches of his resources in this way. He could not express himself in a free and easy way. Every page he wrote, at least for the latter part of his life, was characteristic. Perhaps it is in his purely metaphysical arguments that his unlimited command of words shows itself most marvellously. Yet we are inclined to retract this, and to say that in such sermons as *Tides of the Spirit* he reaches his highest point. In such pieces he seems to surpass every one, living and dead, in the wealth and surprise of his diction. The question which Jeffrey put to Macaulay, 'Where did you get that style?' presses upon us. We venture with diffidence to suggest that it was originally derived from the Scottish philosophers. In his early days he was a warm admirer of Thomas Brown. The reader of to-day will very soon toss Brown aside, but he will not deny that Brown was in his way a great writer. The Scottish philosophers of that period carried philosophical eloquence very far. We need only refer to Dugald Stewart's dissertation in the *Encyclopædia Britannica*, and to Mackintosh's in the same publication. Even the natural philosophers at that time used the arts of style in exposition in a very notable manner. Few more genuinely eloquent writers than Professor Playfair can be found, and there is a true sublimity as well as serenity and clearness in MacLaurin's treatise on the Newtonian discoveries. It may be superseded as a scientific work, but as a masterpiece of expression it still repays study. Yet Martineau's style was by no means unexceptionable. Its stateliness became wearisome. You 'dig for dulness as for hid treasure' in travelling through its incessant eloquence. If the writer could be simple for a moment the effect would be far greater. Nor is it without frequent notes of harshness and untruth. We will take what is perhaps his most admired passage. It occurs in one of his sermons.

> 'Where is it that God, in His searching of the hearts of His children, hears the tones of deepest love, and sees on the uplifted face the light of the most heartfelt gratitude? Not where His gifts are most profuse, but where they seem most meagre; not where the suppliant's worship glides forth from the cushion of luxury through lips satiated with plenty and rounded by health; not within the halls of successful ambition, or even the dwellings of unbroken domestic peace; but where the outcast, flying from persecution, kneels in the evening on the rock whereon he sleeps; by the fresh grave, where, as the earth is opened, Heaven, in answer, opens too; by the pillow of the wasted sufferer, where the sunken eye, denied sleep, converses with a silent star, and the hollow voice enumerates in low prayer, the scanty list of comforts and the shortened tale of hopes.'

How good this is and how bad!

As a philosopher there can be no doubt at all of Martineau's almost unrivalled power. He grappled with his problems until he forced their solution. He grasped the salient facts with the utmost firmness. His thought was subtle, his criticism firm, and his power of exposition and illustration quite unrivalled. He had a most disinterested enthusiasm for the pure truth of philosophy, and, above all, he was a spiritual philosopher, the foremost of our time, perhaps the foremost of his century. Everything went back with him to the supreme idea of moral obligation. From this he deduced the human intellect as apprehending truth and not illusion. Whatever may be thought of his theology, in philosophy he was purely Christian. We cannot think that such a book as *Types of Ethical Theory* can easily be dethroned. It was the result of a lifetime's labour. His steady witness to theism and immortality in face of the vast difficulties raised by evolution was a signal service to the Church of Christ. Many passages come back to the memory, and the first thrill of reading them is renewed. 'Is the eternal design of Perfection to be gained by the frustrated aspirations of countless ephemeral generations? Or to the rule that "One soweth and another reapeth" is there not the compensating sequel, "He that soweth and he that reapeth shall rejoice together"?'

Martineau remained a Christian, but only in the most shadowy sense so far as intellectual belief went. He began in 1836 by denying the Christian name to unbelievers in the recorded miracles of Christ. He ended by denying all miracle, and treating as a moral humiliation the attempt to extract a proof of eternal life from the records of Christ's Resurrection. He held to his own ideal of Christ, not the Christ of the Gospel story, but the Christ whom his own thought fashioned. To him the conceptions of Christ as King, Priest, and

Judge were deforming investitures. But he believed that Christ was a Spirit of sublime fragrance, and even that He was the realised possibility of life in God; but he would not allow that He was more. He would not trust God's revelation as something higher and worthier than man's sense of fitness. He was like a child who would take nothing on the father's authority except what the father could prove to the undeveloped reason and conscience. He so far assimilated modern scientific thought as to rule out miracle in every form as impossible. As a higher critic he showed the most extravagant incredulity. Of his last valuable book, *The Seat of Authority in Matters of Religion*, it has been remarked as 'strange that whenever our Lord's language is at issue with Dr. Martineau's philosophy, the evangelists have been bad reporters.' No great weight is to be attached to his judgments in this kind, for, strictly speaking, he was not a scholar, and never had the chance of being one. But, strange to say, the intensity of his historical scepticism was accompanied with an equal intensity of spiritual devotion which burns especially in his sermons. He never abandoned the possibility and the blessedness of communion with God. The voice obeyed at prime was obeyed at eve—'*Come, my people, enter thou into thy chambers, and shut thy doors about thee: hide thyself as it were for a little moment, until the indignation be overpast.*'

October 30, 1902.

HUGH PRICE HUGHES

THE sudden death of Hugh Price Hughes is to the present writer a keen and disabling personal distress. What it must be to the home circle of which he was the centre and the sun, we hardly dare to think. The Wesleyan Methodist Church has lost one of its most eminent and devoted leaders. But the death is almost the greatest bereavement that could have befallen Nonconformity. Others carry and will continue to carry the banner, but no one can quite take his place. By many years of strenuous and unceasing toil he had gained the ear of England, and upon vast sections of the people he had an unrivalled influence. In the ordinary course of things, he should have been with us to give his fire and counsel for fifteen years more. By the time these years are gone, many issues will be decided. We shall vehemently desire him in the day of battle, but still and always the Leader of faithful souls is with us.

Yet, since we had to lose him, it was better we should lose him so. He was stricken as it were in a moment, and as years count he was hardly past his prime. For months, however, his wonderful energy had been failing. The zeal of God's house had eaten him up. The signals of danger were manifest to his affectionate watchers, even so long as two years ago. He tried to rest, and did rest in some measure, but he could not straighten his back from toil, his ardent spirit could not refrain from the fray. When he returned to his work there were symptoms that gave cause for grave anxiety. But he went on working up to his power and even beyond his power, and he has died in harness, as he would have wished to die. He has been mercifully spared the experience of long inaction, of gradual and hopeless decay. The enthusiasm that burned like lava for so many years has suddenly gone out—for earth and time. On Sunday he preached, on Monday he was writing letters and giving interviews, and his last act was to attend a meeting. Then God's finger touched him, and he fell asleep. It was a death that fitted him, a death to be desired for its surprise and its opportunity. We think of Goethe's words, 'He has the advantage of figuring in the memory of posterity as one eternally able and strong, for the image in which one lives in the world is that in which one moves among the shadows.'

The career of Mr. Hughes, though it seemed short, was in reality long. No life of our time has been more laborious, more consuming. From the night when we first saw him—it was in the Lower Hall of the City Temple, after a lecture—on to the last, it seemed as if he were never a moment still. His preaching, and writing, and speaking, and travelling, and raising money, and fighting, all England knew. Others were aware that he never ceased to give himself away. He had a passion for detail. He loved the work of committees, and never failed to take a leading share in them. It was one of the signs of the end that latterly he would sit quite still and listen to others as they discussed a course of action. He was extremely punctual and methodical in dealing with his vast correspondence. On Saturday we received a letter in his own handwriting, and, indeed, we cannot remember receiving from him any letter that was dictated. Up till a few weeks ago he took great delight in his work for the *Methodist Times*. He was full of matter, and dictated with the utmost ease and relish. Of late, however, he seemed to feel this and other labours a burden. But perhaps his conversation was more remarkable even than his public speaking. We remember no conversationalist quite like him. He was a careful and accurate listener, and at the same time a most copious and eager talker. In this as in other things he seemed always to be parting with vitality. The last time we saw him his eagerness seemed even feverish. His enthusiasm gathered into itself the stress of the nerves and the heat of the blood, and it is no wonder that he died worn out.

Mr. Hughes has not left behind him any mellow and finished literary performance, but his contemporaries know how deeply for the last twenty years he has influenced the Christian life and thought of England. We do not feel competent to describe his work in the great Wesleyan Methodist communion. That its effects were far-reaching every one can see, but only a Methodist can tell how he altered not only the procedure of the Church to which he was so devotedly attached, but even its atmosphere. We prefer to say something about his handling of the larger problems which confront the Christian Churches, and especially the Free Churches. Mr. Hughes came into prominence at a time when it was manifest that Christianity had to face new conditions, and he addressed himself with unbounded hope and courage to the situation.

First of all, he saw that the working classes in this country were becoming alienated from the churches. He saw that the Christian Church had to deal with this life as well as with the next, that the social problem could not be evaded without dereliction of duty and the sacrifice of souls. The time was past when it was enough to preach the peace of a world to come, when men would be content with building for their dark poverty a house not made with hands. The sullen and alienated democracy had to be met upon their own ground. Mr. Hughes did his very best, and perhaps no Christian minister in our time has done more. He perceived that if the workers of the country were to be gathered, the Church must give them the services of her best men and her best buildings. He saw that Nonconformity could never prosper unless its central church in every great town was a church of the poor, a church in which all were equal, a church in which the choicest in every kind was freely given. He perceived also that such churches must have a social side, that the church must lay herself alongside of the whole life of the people week-day and Sunday. But he never made the mistake of supposing that Christianity is to be subordinate to social reform. In the great missions which he directed so long, the preaching of the Gospel came foremost. Mr. Hughes's chief resource, speaking from the human side, was the contagion of a great conviction. No more fervent evangelical addresses were delivered anywhere than the sermons preached by him in St. James's Hall. He did not live to accomplish all that he desired, but he lived long enough to see his policy vindicated. The Wesleyan Methodist Church, through him and others like minded, has led the way. It is more and more clear that other churches will follow. In St. James's Hall he had representatives of all classes in his audience, and he could tell many wonderful stories of the distress and peace of souls under the preaching of himself and his colleague, Mark Guy Pearse. Along with this went an elaborate organisation of social work. In many respects the conditions were such as are not to be found elsewhere in London. Up to the time when his health broke down, Mr. Hughes carried on the mission with unabated success. It was intended, we believe, that he should have charge of the services to be held in the new Church House at Westminster, but so much did he prize the opportunity given by St. James's Hall that he never dreamed of abandoning it. We hope yet to see the system of work which he did so much to establish carried out by all the great denominations in every great town. It will be a most permanent monument to Mr. Price Hughes, for it can never be dissevered from his name and his toil.

Mr. Hughes had also to face the necessary readjustment of Christianity to the changed conditions of thought. Though he was a highly educated man, with a civilised mind, the conditions of his life did not leave him free to become a specialist in any department of knowledge. But he knew what was in the air, and he had to handle the problem as it acutely presented itself in life. He knew that it was necessary to face the questions raised by scholars and scientists. He knew also that even if these difficulties can be dispelled, they are apt to be replaced by others deeper and sadder still, which will not yield to argument. He knew that Christianity has to be presented to the age on a purified, simple, and intelligible basis. Mr. Hughes was not a theological or spiritual adventurer. He was not himself, so far as we are aware, troubled by perplexity. Some things were sure to him, and these were enough. He knew very well how one single thought may keep the soul alive for years. He had much sympathy with mystical depth and religious reverie. The essence of Christianity to him was union with the living Christ. His definition of a Christian was based upon this. We remember his saying that he wished to have written on his tombstone the lines—

> 'Thou, O Christ, art all I want,
> More than all in Thee I find.'

Under the government of this and other kingly thoughts he himself remained undiscouraged and even blithe through all the confusions. He had also a very practical conviction that Christ is Legislator as well as Redeemer, and that obedience is the way to knowledge. His mind, perhaps, had more affinity with the Johannine than with the Pauline writings, but he would have professed himself a loyal Methodist in essentials. We rather think, from recent conversations with him, that on some points of theology he was inclined to go further than he ever said in public. But he had a constant sense of responsibility, and would not speak till he was sure. It will be remembered how at the last Conference he led his brethren in their decision to retain Professor Beet. The decision may have been wise or unwise; we simply note the fact.

The problem which perhaps most distressed Mr. Hughes was that which confronts us to-day—the assault of clericalism on religious liberty. Mr. Hughes had a genuine affection for the Church of England. He had many friends and relations in her communion. At one time he hoped that better and closer relations could be established between the Church of England and Nonconformity. He took a great part in what were known as the Grindelwald Conferences, and resented the very moderate degree of hope with which some of us looked on them. To Episcopacy as a system of Church government he took no objection; in fact, he would not perhaps have been sorry to see the Methodist Episcopal Church of the United States reproduced here. He had a high view of the ministerial profession, and was as rigid as an old Presbyterian in maintaining the clerical garb. But, on the other hand, he abhorred sacerdotalism. He held the Presbyterian view of the Sacraments; beyond that he never went. As time went on, it was forced upon him that the Anglicans would make no concession of any kind. Mr. Hughes was abstractly in favour of Disestablishment, especially Disestablishment in Wales; but he did not take any prominent part in the fight, and in fact was sometimes inclined to discourage it. But he saw that it was advisable that Nonconformity should organise itself, and no one did more to start and support the National Free Church Council. When President of that organisation he delivered an address on the idea of the Church, following pretty closely the lines of Dr. Dale. He successfully prevented the National Free Church Council from taking up the question of Disestablishment. It was his desire to see the Wesleyan Methodists and other Nonconformists working more cordially together, and there can be no doubt that this aim was largely attained. He gave much time and thought to the problem of religious education, and unswervingly supported undenominational teaching. He would, however, have gone so far as to teach the Creed in every school. The Education Bill, under which Nonconformists are to be rated for a Church atmosphere and Church teaching, awoke the deepest hostility of his nature. He saw at once that the only effectual resistance Nonconformists could offer was the resistance of suffering, and was one of the first to advocate the passive resistance policy, which he steadfastly maintained to the end. Through weakness he was unable to do much in the public agitation, but his speech in St. James's Hall will be remembered, and he continued to write in his journal. Mr. Hughes sorrowfully recognised that the Bill had permanently altered the relations between the Church and Nonconformity—that the latter had to defend its life against the former. How far the National Free Church Council will fulfil his hopes will be decided soon. Mr. Hughes had also great hopes of Methodist union, and laboured hard in that cause, but the difficulties so far have proved insurmountable.

In politics he was driven to take an active part, but he was not really a politician. Parties did not interest him as such; it was causes he cared for. In the struggle for Home Rule he was an enthusiastic Gladstonian. Though his zeal cooled, he was always a friend to Ireland, and always convinced that the Irish must be conciliated. To the proposal for a Roman Catholic University he offered a stern opposition. Perhaps the most trying episode of his political career was his support of the South African War. War in itself he hated as much as Arthur Helps hated it. 'Just think for one moment of the agonising night of suffering passed by a wounded man on the field of battle.' He often said that the results of war were very rarely what the promoters of war counted or hoped for. He would have done anything to put his fellow countrymen in love with the ways of peace. Hence it was very painful for him to oppose the anti-war party in this country, especially as many of them had been amongst his closest friends. Having persuaded himself, however, that the war was a war of defence on our part, and not a war of aggression, he did not flinch from saying so. He encountered a storm of opposition, but met it with perfect good temper. The little brush between him and Sir Henry Campbell-Bannerman need not be recalled, but it is no breach of confidence now to say that at the private meeting between Sir Henry Campbell-Bannerman and the Nonconformists Mr. Price Hughes took the lead in expressing, with the utmost good nature and good feeling, his earnest desire that bygones should be bygones, and that unity among Liberals should be restored. The response was as gracious as the speech that prompted it.

We have no space to write of the qualities that so eminently fitted Mr. Hughes for his work. Foremost among them was his deep piety. Nobody knew him at all who did not recognise that he was profoundly religious. The lower ambitions he plucked out and cast from him. He was delivered from the love of money and the love of ease. Nothing entered his life that was not penetrated by his passion for Christ. Even when one did not quite understand him one was sure that he was following the lines :—

> 'The loftiest spirits in their wildest motion
> Dip to their anchors underneath the ocean.'

His courage was based on faith. Faith, it has been said, once could shake mountains; mountains now shake faith. Mountains never shook his faith. He was extraordinarily alert and swift. As a manager of meetings he could not be surpassed. Those who were present at the great gathering where he denounced Parnell in face of a large hostile element will never forget the scene. As a speaker he was not one of the masters of an eloquence enhanced by

> 'that great voice which, rising, brought
> Red wrath to faces pale with thought,
> And, falling, fell with showers of tears.'

But the *Times* has rightly said that he was one of the six most popular speakers in England. He was always clear, direct, and full of life. Though he was a born fighter, and always in controversy, there was no bitterness in his nature. We doubt if he was ever guilty of a cruel and wounding personal remark. We say this who have fought him, and who have watched his battles with others. In private conversation he was the same. There is not a word we ever heard him say of any human being which might not be written down and published. All who really knew him know the inherent kindness, gentleness, and generosity of his nature, and the intense tenderness of his domestic affections. Then he was practically sagacious in the highest degree. He knew what he longed for, what he wished to do. He had the gift of getting things done. He often appeared to be intemperate in expression, but this was not really so. He had an exaggerated way of speaking. Every hour was regal to him. But his nature was cautious and conservative, and he had all the attributes of a great general. He did not know how to take care of himself, and so to-day multitudes mourn and miss him, and will continue to miss him all the time between the digging of his grave and theirs. But it is ours to remember that he who lies dead to-day was a good soldier of Jesus Christ; one who did not take counsel of meaner fears; one who was tried and bore the test; one who was eager to welcome great experiences; one who said with his whole heart, *Even so come, Lord Jesus*. We were not blind to all that when he was near to us in the flesh; we see it more clearly now.

November 20, 1902.

DR. PARKER

To estimate aright a personality so great, so complex, and so many-sided as that of Dr. Parker, is a task so difficult that I shrink from attempting it. Nor is it necessary to record in detail the few outstanding events of his public life. The stern but victorious struggle of his youth, his pastorate of five years in Banbury, his conspicuous ministry in Manchester for eleven years, and his world-known work in London for the long period of thirty-three years, have been fully described by himself and others. I shall rather try to picture him as he appeared to me during the last years of his life, when I saw much of him. It is, as yet, impossible to imagine that he is dead—impossible to associate the thought of death with a vitality so exuberant. He believed himself that his strength began to fail at the time he delivered his address as Chairman of the Congregational Union in the Manchester Free Trade Hall. But he had boundless faith in his physical resources, in his power of recovery, and cherished the hope of restoration till very near the end. Dr. Parker believed himself that his illness was a mystery even to his physicians. I suppose, however, that he died of no specific disease. His magnificent energy was worn out, the heart ceased to fulfil its proper functions, and refused to answer stimulants. All his life he had been pouring out his force into his work, and the intense strain of soul and body from which he suffered before and after his great bereavement, could not but sap his strength. Yet it is but a few weeks ago since he went back to his pulpit with, as it seemed, the fresh hope of young life in his veins. He preached with unabated power, and looked forward to years of work. When at last it became evident that there was little hope, he faced the end with a heroic yet sad composure. He loved his life, and he loved his labour. But his sufferings were so great that he craved release, and almost sued for the mercy of death. He bore his burden with wonderful patience, and though he spoke not much of religion when dying, he said his Amen to God's will. Among his last signs of life was the response he gave to favourite hymns like 'My faith looks up to Thee,' and 'There is a fountain filled with blood.' It is impossible for human nature to look on the end of such a life without pain, but there are weighty consolations. It was very hard to witness his sufferings, so hard that the affectionate watchers by his deathbed longed for his release. His life was not maimed as so many lives seem to be. His longings were high and noble, and in large measure fulfilled. He found his true path in life, and he followed it without weariness and without failure till death was in sight. He was not condemned to live in the prison of a paralysed body. The note of disappointment which echoes from all the winds is less audible in his career than in almost any we can call to mind. He never swerved from the firm conviction that he was called to serve God in the Nonconformist ministry, and there was never an hour when he would have changed his work for any other in the world.

I shall try to set out simply the course of his days. While the tributes to his memory have been almost always kind and well-intentioned, many stories told in them are entirely without foundation. His way of living was very regular, very methodical, and very simple. Every morning he was in his study at half-past seven, and spent his first half hour looking at the newspapers. After breakfast he retired to his study, and dealt immediately with his correspondence. He answered letters either at once or not at all. He reserved to himself the right to ignore unreasonable requests and complaints, but his charity was great, and he could not easily resist appeals for aid. He then went on with reading or literary work for a couple of hours. Afterwards he walked, invariably alone. It was during his walks that he loved to meditate his sermons; and he might be seen any day on Hampstead Heath absorbed in contemplation, and sometimes with his lips moving. In the evening he loved to be read to. Hour after hour he would listen, and if he liked a book he had it read over to him again. He retired to rest early after his simple meal, and this was the routine of his days. Though he lived in a handsome modern house, and had everything well appointed, he was eminently frugal and homely in his habits. Dr. Parker's charity was very great. He did not care to speak of it, but he was unable entirely to conceal it. I doubt whether I have known any man who habitually gave away a larger share of his income. At the same time the straits which he went through in his early life had made him careful, and though he was generous, he never wasted money. Few men have cared less for general society. He liked to meet people in whom he was interested, and sometimes accepted invitations, but no man in a similar position ever went out so little. When he did accept an invitation to a dinner-party, he was always miserable before he went, and often miserable after. He would imagine that he had said something or done something that should not have been said or done. Yet he liked to think and speak of the famous people whom he had met. What is much more remarkable, Dr. Parker had at no time in his life any special genius for friendship. Those nearest him, those who have known him best and longest, bear witness with one voice to this. He was full of friendliness, but till the days of his loneliness he did not need close friends. That craving for fellowship which has characterised so many was not his, even in his early days. His was essentially a lonely nature, much occupied in brooding, and in musing, far withdrawn. On the other hand, he had a more than common delight in the fellowship of his home. The society of his wife and her relatives and a few more seemed to satisfy his wants. He loved to have visits from his own inner circle. Even then, however, he spent much of his time alone, though he liked to know that his wife was in the house, and was restless and uneasy in her absence. He needed also the stimulus of the great crowds he preached to three times in the week. Between his congregation and his home his life was practically lived until his wife died. After that he turned very strongly to two or three friends who visited him every week. In general company he had little to say, but among his own, and especially in dialogue, he was at his very best. As a rule he wakened up slowly, but once embarked in the full stream of conversation, he was vivacious and brilliant to an extraordinary degree. He then showed himself a man of genius. I have met men cleverer and more accomplished, and even men more alert, but never a man, with perhaps one exception, more plainly possessed of the indefinable quality called genius. In conversation he could adapt himself to his companion, but, latterly at least, he liked nothing so well as to discuss his texts with a sympathetic hearer, or to recall his memories of the past. He would often speak with the utmost finish, precision, and beauty. To set down one's memory of his sentences would only be to mar them. No man was ever more concerned with his own special work, but his method of preparing his sermons was his own. He read much in the Bible, and texts started out of its pages. When he found a text he brooded over it in his solitary walks, in his study, and in his garden, till he reached the heart of it. Once that was discovered, illustrations crowded upon him, and his work was practically done. There lie before me as I write many of his sermon notes used in the pulpit. They are written in pencil, and each text is followed by about a dozen lines. This was quite enough for him. His preaching was never at any time a burden to him, but always a joy. He was very rarely in need of a text; in fact, he had almost always a few texts in hand. Dr. Parker's thoughts all concentrated themselves on his pulpit work, and on his Sunday morning sermons especially. When he was in the pulpit all was well with him. The crowd roused and stimulated all his faculties. There was no want of words, and the words came as at the command of a magician, arranging themselves in forms of startling beauty and freshness. He forgot his own sentences as soon as they were spoken, and could not recognise them when they were quoted to him again. It was rarely if ever that he repeated a sentence or a phrase. He was not, in my opinion, a good judge of his own work, but in his preaching he was notably equal, though some subjects naturally fitted him better than others. There was no abatement in his pulpit power, but rather the reverse. Perhaps as time went on he became more aphoristic and sententious, but of this I am not sure. His power of attraction grew with the advancing years, and at a time when most preachers are repeating themselves, he was ever striking out new lines of thought and expression. He would say, however, that young preachers ought to write their sermons, and that he himself had written carefully for years. On the rare occasions when he wrote and read a sermon, he was much less effective, and as a rule his appearances on great occasions were much below his average. Of this he was very well aware. The only time I ever knew him decidedly fail was in his speech at the Union of the Churches in Scotland. He failed simply because he had prepared too much. For months the speech ran in his mind, until at last he lost confidence in himself. No one ever preached more earnestly the absolute necessity of labour and concentration for any success in the pulpit, and he practised all he preached.

Dr. Parker was extremely sensitive. Perhaps sensitiveness goes much more often with genius than with talent. He greatly lacked self-confidence, and lived in the constant need of encouragement. The occasional brusqueness and egotism of his manner was in reality a mask of shyness, for he remembered with marvellous tenacity all who had shown him any kindness. He never forgot to be grateful. His was a nature that had much need of brightness, and he would often pray for some visible sign or token that he was doing good. He had himself a generous admiration for every kind of excellence in the old and in the young. The two men, I think, whom he admired most were Dr. Maclaren and Principal Rainy, and their visits in his sickness gave him peculiar delight. But it need not be denied that this sensitiveness, almost grotesque at times, led him into much trouble. As a rule, he did not read attacks upon himself, but when he read them he could hardly be restrained from replying to them, no matter how puny the assailant might be. He had even the weakness of seeing allusions to himself which were never meant as such, and in this way he suffered needless pain. It was difficult for him to believe that he was loved. He could not take it upon trust. He had to be told it over and over again. In his later years he mellowed greatly, but the story of his life is in one aspect a record of struggle and combat, and its peace was marred by needless misunderstandings. Struggle and combat may be the happiest conditions under which a man can exist, but it would have been well for Dr. Parker if he had given more trust alike to himself and to others. He was often taken for an enormous egoist, and in a sense that was true. His thoughts were much concentrated on himself and his own work, but no one judged himself more humbly, no one was more vulnerable to unkindness, no one was more easily shaken by a breath of adverse criticism.

This sensitiveness was caused, I have no doubt,

by the hardness of his childhood and youth. He said once that his life had been a continual fight and a frequent pain. It was true that his career was hewn out by stress of will. Every sixpence he possessed was earned. He won and kept his own position against hosts of adversaries. His impulsiveness and his sensitiveness cost him much. They prevented him from being a really great leader. He could take up a cause and fight for it, but it was hard for him to differ from those he cared for, and harder still to hold on through storm and darkness and defeat, looking confidently for long and far results. On the great questions that have divided Liberalism in the last twenty years he wavered, changed his views from time to time, and latterly he shrunk wisely from committing himself. He would take up a cause and grow weary of it, and turn to something else. On all but the great subjects his mind was restless, and he would seek for premature and impossible reconciliations. Yet, as I have said, he had much happiness, and in the old days I believe his spirits were often exuberant. He was always grateful for his life, though he never wished to live any part of it over again.

Dr. Parker, through all his career, was firmly and consistently evangelical and Nonconformist. Through all his years and labours there ran the intense unwavering sense of Christ's redeeming care. For him Christ was the Alpha and Omega, the Beginning and the End, the First and the Last.

His strong influence had its source in a hidden life. He was deeply, humbly, and fervently religious. He was before all things a preacher of the Christian redemption, living and dying under the benediction of the Cross. With works of systematic theology he had small acquaintance, but he was mighty in the Scriptures, and never was the Bible read more earnestly and believingly than by him. By his own study and thought he had worked out independently all the main conclusions of evangelicalism and he never moved away from them. In the same way, he was a convinced and consistent Nonconformist. Where Nonconformists were divided he would hesitate, and move sometimes from one side to another, but though he received much kindness from members of the Church of England, and was most grateful for it, he had no sympathy at all for the Anglican position. Indeed it often struck me that he did not understand how much can be said for sacerdotal views, though I do not forget *Springdale Abbey*. Everything in the shape of ceremonial and external religion was intensely repugnant to his nature. He so much disliked the undue estimate of the Sacraments that he did not give them their due, and would have agreed with Dr. Bruce that it would be well if for a time they were abandoned. He attached his own meaning to Baptism and the Lord's Supper, looking upon them as beautiful symbolic acts, but he did not believe that either did anything to strengthen the life of the Church. He vehemently maintained that any one might preside over the Lord's Supper, and said that he would rather receive the emblems from the hands of his own mother than from those of many ministers. His Nonconformity took shape in the old strenuous days of the Church Rate fights, and he loved to tell how his father's furniture was sold, because he would not pay. It was natural he should be one of the first to suggest resistance to the new Church Rate, and on this his mind dwelt much. Dr. Parker was convinced that the present crisis, if bravely met, would be the rebirth of Nonconformity. He had a certain pity for Nonconformists who went over to the Church. For himself the desertion of the cause to which he was bound by ties so dear would have been an act of spiritual suicide.

Dr. Parker's literary achievements, apart from the pulpit, are not memorable. He had an ambition to write novels, and there was undoubtedly a deep vein of romance and tenderness in his nature, notwithstanding its rugged virility. There are fine passages in *Springdale Abbey* and *Raven Digby* amid much that is unsatisfactory. He had journalistic ambitions also, but the truth is that he did not work hard enough and long enough either at fiction or at journalism to achieve any real success. He almost always grew weary of a book long before he had finished it, and eked it out with passages from former books. *Ecce Deus* and the *Paraclete* were works on which he spent much labour, and they had a certain success. But the fact is he was too deeply pledged to preaching to win any real triumph in other fields.

It was as a preacher that he made his great mark and exerted his mighty influence. For multitudes there was no preacher like him. He showed power from the first, but he took bad models, and his taste was imperfect. It is wonderful to trace his progress, to see how he toiled and how he ascended. To other preachers he owed almost nothing. The one preacher whose influence is traceable in his later work is Newman, and Newman was almost the only sermon writer whom he read for many years. I make no attempt to analyse his preaching, or to discover the secret of his power. It was a spiritual wonder. There was about it the touch of miracle. Apparently free from rule, it was unconsciously obedient to the great principles of art. As you listened you saw deeper meanings. The horizon lifted, widened, broadened —the preacher had thrust his hand among your heart strings. You heard the cry of life, and the Christ preached as the answer to that cry. The preacher had every gift. He was mystical, poetical, ironical, consoling, rebuking by turns. Sometimes

> 'As from an infinitely distant land,
> Come airs and floating echoes that convey
> A melancholy into all our day.'

The next moment you could not help smiling at some keen witticism. Then he was ironical, and you remembered Heine, and saw that he knew how much irony is mingled by God in the order of His creation. Then tears sprang to your eyes as he pictured the failure of success, and told of the long, triumphant struggle and the victory turned into mourning by the death of the only child. But what description can render, or what analysis explain, the visible inspiration, the touch of fire from heaven ?

Dr. Parker's last days were shadowed by his great bereavement in the death of the wife whose loyal affection had sustained him through all the storm and struggle of thirty-four years. When her call came she heard it long before he would listen, and was always very calm and very brave. He controlled himself in her presence, but when he left her he would break into fits of passionate weeping. He never could bear leave-takings. When visitors stayed in his house he never said good-bye, and never liked to know when they were going. He had asked his wife in their early days of marriage to promise that they would never say farewell to one another, and the promise was kept. Death was to him the most formidable of foes, and he would say, 'When I come to die do not preach to me, do not exhort me—leave me with myself and with God.' His wife had an exulting faith in immortality. Dr. Parker himself, for many years, was most curiously fascinated by the idea of corporate immortality. It was not by any means that he disbelieved in individual immortality, but much was dark to him on that side. He viewed the life after death for long with hesitations and tremors, and fought his battle in many sad, long, quiet hours after his wife was gone. Scrupulously truthful and sincere in every expression of feeling, he said nothing of reunion for long. His mind imperatively rejected the commonplace and the sentimental. The unknown and untried regions which the spirit enters when it is severed from the flesh daunted him. But the mists lifted. As the end drew near his faith became clearer, and the hope of reunion seemed to shed a soft radiance and illumination over his worst sufferings, a soothing sense of repose and hope.

December 4, 1902.

DR. GEORGE MATHESON

It is not the night but the light that has fallen on the strenuous, brave life of Dr. George Matheson. In him we have lost one of the most chivalrous spirits of our time, one who lived as he taught, faithfully and nobly. The dimmed and hindered body in which he did his work has been laid reverently in its last resting-place till the trumpet shall sound, but he himself is where the pleroma of the universe has become luminous. He has received a house from heaven where they who look out at the windows are not darkened.

It was Dr. Matheson's characteristic way to make as little as possible of his affliction. The trial was one of the hardest that can fall to a human being. In his early days as a schoolboy and a student, he was the most brilliant of his compeers, and when he was only twenty there fell upon him the dire calamity of blindness. He would not suffer it to break his spirit. When, in 1899, he took farewell of his Edinburgh congregation, he described himself as 'barred by every gate of fortune, yet refusing to give in; overtaken by the night, yet confident of the morning.' He said: 'My sermons may have flown over your heads like the bird of paradise, but my life has been level to yours—an obstructed life, a circumscribed life, but a life of boundless sanguineness, a life of quenchless hopefulness, a life which has beaten persistently against the cage of circumstance, and which even at the time of abandoned work has said not "Good night," but "Good morning."' We may not judge the love so darkly wise that ordained his lot any more than he did, but it is impossible not to think of what he might have done in the ordinary conditions. George Matheson, we verily believe, was potentially the greatest man given to the Scottish Churches since the days of Dr. Chalmers. He was a great orator, a powerful thinker, a man born with the instinct of scholarship, a master of expression, overflowing with love and vehement ardour, and dauntless courage. Such a man might have had Scotland at his feet, and he would certainly have been one of the rulers of the spiritual empire. In spite of all, he did great things, but the greatest of all was the living of his life. There can be no doubt that the natural course of his intellectual development was seriously disturbed by his infirmity. In his devotional writings, as in all devotional writings of real mark, we sometimes overhear the author. It would not be right, it would not be fair, it would not be considerate to point out what is overheard. He himself made no complaint; but to him it was easier a great deal to die than to live. We will try to point out the strange course of his mental and spiritual history, though this can be done only in a very imperfect manner. Where he was reticent we must not be too confident.

The first time we saw Dr. Matheson must have been somewhere about 1880. He was delivering the second of the Baird lectures on a Sunday evening in St. George's, Edinburgh. The great building was but scantily filled, but the address, alike in matter, in form, and in utterance, was worthy of any audience. It seemed as if we had in Dr. Matheson the coming prophet of the time. His face was turned with eager welcome towards the new light, and his strong brain was busy in the work of reconstruction and reconciliation. When the sermon was over, we went to the Synod Hall and heard the latter part of an oration by Principal Cairns. This was a grand defence of the old apologetical positions delivered with overwhelming passion, and uncompromising in its orthodoxy. That evening was indeed spent well and nobly. We had heard the fittest representatives of the old school and of the new. But it was not as a philosophical thinker but as a devotional writer that Dr. Matheson was to win his fame.

I

Before he was blind, he distinguished himself in philosophy, and later on he came under the powerful influence of John Caird. His attainments were very considerable, and he went on adding to them to the utmost of his power. It was as a scientific theologian and as a scholar that he first made his appeal to the public. In 1874 he issued his first book, *Aids to the Study of German Theology*, and in 1877 there appeared in two volumes what was perhaps his most elaborate work, *The Growth of the Spirit of Christianity, from the First Century to the Dawn of the Lutheran Era.* The publication of that book seemed to close an epoch in his life. It was a very able and thoughtful work, the result of wide and well-directed reading. But it had weaknesses which were perhaps inevitable. We do not specially refer to the somewhat fantastic analogy drawn between the mental growth of a man and that of the Christian Church. Dr. Matheson assigned places to St. Paul and St. Augustine in the 'child life.' The 'school life' ended with the Council of Constance, and then followed 'the independence of youth,' which closed with the appearance of Luther. The inference drawn was that the period from Luther to the present day is the manhood of the Christian Church. It is needless to make any comment. Dr. Matheson made a bold and not unsuccessful attempt to show how the free teaching of the earliest ages passed into scholasticism, and how scholasticism was dethroned. In the course of his discussion he said much that was suggestive, but also much that was open to criticism. For example, he wrote, 'Reason is given to China, imagination to India, understanding to Egypt, and will to Persia. With Greece there begins the reconciliation of that which was destroyed, and at length in Christianity the reconstruction is complete and the human race resumes its original position as a united and harmonious family.' We believe he came to see that there is something quite unconvincing about these characterisations. How should China have reason, and Egypt understanding? and how can it be said that the human race is united and harmonious? But the point on which his ablest critics fastened was the number of small inaccuracies in the volume. One reviewer pointed out some of his mistakes, and brought against him the general charge that he lacked accurate knowledge. 'Mr. Matheson makes odd blunders in small matters, which seem to show that he is not an accurate student.' Little do reviewers know the circumstances in which books are written. If that reviewer had understood that the author of the book was a blind man, he would have expressed himself differently. But Dr. Matheson was from first to last resolutely determined to claim no immunity and no indulgence on account of his blindness. If by reason of that blindness he could not adequately fulfil any particular part, he would withdraw from the attempt. When he saw that for the purposes of scholarship his blindness was a fatal hindrance, he withdrew from the field—not without pangs, but finally.

II

The next step of his work was that of an apologist. He conceived that he might be still able to do something in harmonising the old faith with the new. At that time the young theological thinkers of Scotland were breaking through the barriers of the old orthodoxy. The Broad Church party had established itself in the Church of Scotland, and Robertson Smith had begun his revolutionary work in the Free Church. Evolution and the Higher Criticism had come to stay. It was a testing time. We remember one evolutionist telling how, at a period when the *Recreations of a Country Parson* and the sermons of Henry Ward Beecher furnished him the food which delighted his soul, he came in contact with Darwin. The new philosophy fell on the orderly line of his mental evolution like a shell, blasting and wrecking it. He had to begin all over again, and discover the ideal anew, both in the mind and in the world. The sentence of Huxley kept ringing in his ears, 'Extinguished theologians lie about the cradle of every science like the strangled snakes about that of Hercules.' It seemed for the moment as if theology itself were the great snake and science the Hercules that had destroyed its life. The sentence sounded like Louis XIV.'s 'There are no more Pyrenees.' But the Pyrenees exist and theology exists. Then Robertson Smith, clinging fondly to the Calvinistic theology of his Church, expounded the processes and results of the Higher Criticism as applied to the Old Testament. What was left of the Bible when the critical process attained its completion? These were the questions which young Matheson confronted, and he did so at the beginning in a most sanguine spirit. When we first became personally acquainted with him, he was full of such subjects. The religious bearings of the doctrine of evolution engrossed his mind. We remember him expressing his great admiration of Liddon's apologetic work, and his conviction that some Broad Churchmen had yielded more than they needed to yield. The fruits of his thought were given in various books, among them *Can the Old Faith Live with the New?* published in 1885, and the *Psalmist and the Scientist,* in 1887. The latter work was hailed in the pages of *The British Weekly* by Professor Elmslie. Dr. Matheson was keenly alive to the spiritual perplexities of his time. He knew the changed conditions under which the Church had to do its work, but he had no fear. He was confident that he could establish the intellectual coherence of religious and scientific truth. He was alive to the fact that a sinister divorce had taken place between faith and science; that the main advances of reason had been made outside the borders of the Church; and that immense departments of new knowledge and experience had grown up unreconciled to her creed. The hostile forces seemed to have with them the powers of the new world—the reason, the knowledge, the criticism of the coming age. He took the field desiring to welcome the truth from every quarter, and persuaded that no truth could contradict or impair the Christian religion.

III

But as time went on he seemed to lose his confidence. On this subject we must speak with caution, for he has not said much about his trial.

Suffice it to say that he came to disbelieve in the Higher Criticism and in the doctrine of evolution, at least in its extreme form. He even came to the conclusion that a new revelation would be given to keep the Church alive. Dr. Matheson was one who could never have forsaken Christianity as he had received it. There are those who in perplexity part from the Church, deeply as they feel the moral beauty of its precepts and the greatness of its work. There are those who nominally remain in the Church while adopting a form of Christianity bereft alike of mystery and of power. Dr. Matheson could do neither. He abandoned the difficulties with which his searching intellect and his deep heart had vainly grappled, and turned his face to the spiritual East. Since then his books have all been essentially devotional books. He set himself to live more truly the life that is hid with Christ in God. For ourselves, we do not doubt that the harmony of all truth is already to be discerned, though for many reasons the complete reconciliation must be slowly accomplished. Dr. Matheson made his choice and contributed his part. He turned his face towards Sion. He proved and proved again the reality of the spiritual light. To him the East was not silent and relentless. The dayspring from on high visited him more and more gloriously, and the finest book he ever wrote is his *Studies of the Portrait of Christ.* Even in the darkness of this world the kindly light was about his feet and on his face. He was strengthened to the end and strengthened many by the ancient succours of the soul.

We linger as we recall him—his cheery cordiality, his zest of appreciation, his large and winning charity. We met him first at the Presbyterian Council in Belfast some twenty years ago, and attended with him many of the meetings. How frank and refreshing were his criticisms! One night Dr. Stalker gave one of his finest addresses, and it seemed as if Dr. Matheson could not cease analysing it and praising it. After many attempts to characterise it justly, he satisfied himself by saying it was truly on the model of Aristotle! At that Council an American Presbyterian minister, long dead now—Dr. G. P. Hays, of Denver—made the most successful, witty, and tactful of chairmen. Dr. Matheson was so pleased with him that he insisted on being present all the time he was in the chair, and at night he recounted, with his marvellous memory, every good thing the American had said. Dr. Matheson was a firmly attached member of the Church of Scotland, and a strong supporter of her position; but he delighted in everything that was excellent wherever he found it, and attached small importance to mere churchmanship. So the radiance of his nature mastered the darkness of time. He was indeed one of the most brotherly and generous of men. 'Might we meet when twilight has become day!'

September 6, 1906.

PRINCIPAL RAINY

Dr. Rainy was one of the greatest of Churchmen, and the name of his Church was deeply graven upon his heart. Her solicitudes occupied his last waking moments. He, we may be sure, was not one of the exiles who needed Jeremiah's precept, 'Let Jerusalem come into your mind.' Jerusalem had been in his mind, his thought by day, his dream by night this many a long year. But to those who saw him of late years it was evident that he who had carried the cross of the earthly Jerusalem, prayed for her peace, toiled for her triumph, had let the heavenly Jerusalem come much into his mind. He was watching for the great door to open and the welcoming angels to beckon. The nearest and the dearest had gone first. The fourscore years were over; life was by the day and hour, and the mother city was smiling down on the old pilgrim. He was to go to Jerusalem out of Galilee, and it mattered little from what port he should sail into the Fair Havens.

'Is the almond blossom bitter?
  Is the grasshopper heavy to bear?
Christ make me happier, fitter
  To go to my own over there:
Jerusalem the Golden,
  What bliss beyond compare.

'My Lord, where I have offended
Do Thou forgive it me,
That so, when, all being ended,
I hear Thy last decree,
I may go up to Jerusalem
Out of Galilee.'

To us it seems that there is no sadness here, no tragic story of unfulfilled hope and life broken off in its beginning, no repetition of the many-toned disappointment which echoes from all the winds. Nothing of that, but a life spent well and nobly, a life that buckled itself early to a great work, and never failed to thrill in every vein to the inspirations of faith and hope. He has heard the great decree which they have heard who have been already taken and sanctified. He has gone with them up to Jerusalem out of Galilee.

I

We foresee that there will always be some difficulty in bringing home to succeeding generations the greatness of Principal Rainy. Those who knew him and had watched his ways will all say that there never was a human being through whose nature there rang more distinctly the note of personal greatness. That was the word. Others exceeded him easily in various qualities; but he excelled in that. We cannot argue from his books, and we could not in his lifetime always reason with confidence from his sermons or addresses. He would be at the least well worth listening to, but there were more potent authors and more masterful orators. Those who wished to know Principal Rainy had to see him at the head of the Free Church Assembly. Like Pompilia in *The Ring and the Book*, Dr. Rainy had each year his 'great fortnight.' This was the fortnight during which his Assembly met to discuss the affairs of the Church. Very likely when the Assembly met there were complaints about some of his doings, there were possibly little jealousies and conspiracies, though we do not know of them. He had against him a strong body of conservatives of whom one at least was a foeman quite worthy of his steel—the late Dr. Begg. But this man sat quietly at his table taking notice of everything, apparently unwilling to move, the least eager of all leaders. The business went on, and things, as they always do, became mixed. Then every one turned to that silent figure. The more difficult the business was, the more eagerly and imperatively they turned. But there was no question on which opinion was divided on which men did not wish to hear the view of Principal Rainy. It might be a question of order, it might be a question of good manners, it might be something that bore on the relations of a minister with his congregation, it might be something far wider and weightier. Whatever it was, all looked to Rainy, and he would in due season rise up and in his stately, calm, quiet, adequate way set forth his view of the case. The view almost invariably commended itself to the house. So great did his power become, that on one occasion, we remember when some question had to be decided, and it was discovered that Rainy was not in the house, the Assembly quietly adjourned to wait for his opinion. This extraordinary action was taken by a body of able men, not a few of them very able, most of them fully convinced of their own power to transact business. But Rainy was the leader, always drawing up resolutions, motions, admonitions and the like, and always with his finger on the pulse of the house. He gave an extraordinary impression of wisdom. Here was a wise man; take heed to him. Nor can it be doubted that he was a wise man, and wise not only as a great man of the world is wise, but with a wisdom that was rooted very deep. He was more than adequate for all the work of a leader. When he saw it to be safe he could laugh away a matter of threatening aspect. As a debater none was cooler or more ready. When a great speech had to be made, it was generally forthcoming, and it was always forthcoming if the call for it was primarily moral. The atmosphere in that old hall suited him perfectly. It called out all his best qualities. He was absolutely at home; he did himself justice there as he never perhaps did elsewhere. There was about him an element of inertia, and the quickening impulse of the Assembly was just enough to break the spell. We appeal to those who have watched Dr. Rainy through these weeks to confirm us when we say that those who accepted his leadership in the Free Church Assembly were perfectly certain that in any deliberative assembly in the world he would have taken the same place. He would have been the first man in no time. His ambitions were not great perhaps, and he would cheerfully have stood aside for any one he believed in, but the mass of mankind love to be led. They like nothing so well as to have a man whom they can trust, who speaks for them, who acts for them. The power of leadership is extraordinarily rare. Where it exists it is often seriously marred by untrustworthiness, by impulse, by passion manifesting itself variously. In Rainy's case this was not so. He was perfectly self-controlled; he was incapable of mean retaliations, and his hand when he lifted it was very heavy. If Dr. Rainy had been a member of the House of Commons, he would most certainly have been the first man there, and it would have been so in the House of Lords or anywhere else. This was a born ruler of men, and much greater in a deliberative assembly than anywhere else.

It might appear as if the leadership of the Free Church Assembly was a limited sphere, but it never seemed so to him. He was heart and soul with the Free Church, the grateful recipient of its first enthusiasms, of its championships, of its ideals. The eagerness with which he accepted the whole Disruption doctrine was very wonderful, and what was more wonderful still was the fact, we think undoubted, that he retained it with very little modification to the last. In his final years, when he could smile at some old battles, he was very loth to admit anything against the Disruption heroes. Through all the storms of his time he carried the old evangelical theology. We should be very much surprised to hear that he ever admitted in public the errancy of Holy Scripture in any part. On one occasion he spoke vehemently in private about certain methods of New Testament criticism. He said, 'The man who believes that any nameless forger could have written a book like the Epistle to the Ephesians or any part of it, is a man entirely outside of my comprehension.' We say he loved the principles of the Church, and he loved the Church equally. He knew the whole body north and south. Highland himself, for he was essentially a Highland gentleman, he delighted in the Highland ministers, and in the Lowlands all doors were open to him. He took his work in hand cheerfully, and gradually obtained concessions to liberalism such as hymn-singing and the like. But the prejudices against hymns and organs did not seem to him unreasonable or vexatious. He considered them with patient care, and was not shocked or at least would not admit he was shocked, when a famous friend declared that if organs were introduced to churches there was no barrier to the re-establishment of the Levitical system in all its fulness!

II

So much for Rainy in his own Church. There he attained as much success as can be expected by any human being, but it is vain to deny that there was another side to his life. Superbly prosperous in winning his own men, he was very much less successful in obtaining the confidence and overcoming the hostility of those who were outside and opposed to him. Perhaps there was no ecclesiastical leader more bitterly attacked and more sincerely disliked than Dr. Rainy. It is not easy to explain this, but something may be said.

When Rainy was a young minister in the north, a fellow-presbyter, a man of delightful innocence, was asked his opinion of the youth. He replied: 'Mr. Rainy is a truly devout young man, but has great difficulty in expressing himself.' There is something in this—a quaintness, a salt—which has kept it alive in our mind. In a sense Dr. Rainy had very great difficulty in expressing himself. It was often very hard to follow him. A golden mist hung over his words—sometimes it was a leaden mist. All the Scottish humorists did their best. 'Dr. Rainy was misty as well as Rainy,' gave satisfaction for a time. But his own men did not resent this. They accepted perhaps the familiar explanation that their want of apprehension was a mere evidence that the thought of the speaker had its spring in a region quite above the mind of the hearer. They saw that he himself was intense, earnest, and spiritual. His glimpses were to them more precious than clear logical demonstrations.

Some two years ago we read with great care the whole of the discussions on union in the Free Church

Assembly from 1865 to 1875. They represented the best men of the Church, and no one could deny that the case of both sides was effectively stated. One series of speeches, however, was very far above the rest, both intellectually and morally. The speaker had the power of marshalling his arguments in the most telling way, and above all, he never ran away from any argument. These speeches were by Sir Henry Moncreiff. Rainy's speeches as a whole had little bearing on the real points under discussion, but they were redeemed by a certain noble vision of what the Church might be. We have no doubt that Rainy was rapturously listened to where Moncreiff was heard with decorous patience. This is proof to our mind that obscurity may be a great power in a speaker, notwithstanding Sir George Cornewall Lewis. Sir George Lewis wrote: 'If we were asked what is the first and second and third qualification of any English statesman we would answer Intelligibility. As in oratory the most eloquent words and the wisest counsels will avail but little if they are not impressed by voice and manner on the minds of an audience; so integrity and public spirit will fail to command confidence if the course adopted is intricate and inexplicable.' Dr. Rainy never had the gift of lucidity, but undoubtedly as time went on he took a certain pleasure in his own power of innocent mystification. The result was very bad. Opponents were exasperated. They became persuaded that Dr. Rainy was an astute and crafty ecclesiastic, with a double meaning in all he said. The extraordinary series of attacks on him published in the *Scotsman* for many years have probably no parallel in journalism. We doubt whether Dr. Rainy gave them any attention. If he satisfied his own people, the other counted for nothing. Was this right ? We cannot think so. Sometimes a church has at her centre a great, benignant, fatherly figure, a Chalmers or a Norman Macleod, who by the mere warmth of his glowing life softens asperity and banishes suspicion at every turn. We believe that the great ecclesiastic of the future will do his very utmost to understand the position of his opponents. Dr. Rainy was satisfied with the Free Church. He was not even anxious to promote a reconciliation between the Church and culture. He himself was a man whose reading took unexpected turns ; we remember in the height of the Church case receiving from him a long quotation copied from the last book of Anatole France. But though during his leadership much was done to develop Free Church literature, it was not done by him. He showed himself, for example, singularly indifferent about the loss of a man like Robertson Smith. Robertson Smith had been his pupil and admired him very much, but Rainy thought him impossible. When Dr. Rainy had his famous controversy with Dean Stanley, it was reviewed by Mr. Rauwenhoff in the *Theologisch Tijdschrift.* Robertson Smith summarised this review in the *British and Foreign Evangelical Review* for January 1873. After mentioning that Rauwenhoff regarded the controversy as parallel to that going on in Holland between the Modern party and the orthodox school, he went on :—

'He is quite at one with Dr. Rainy in regarding the Dean's lectures, not as a contribution to Church history, but an apology for Moderatism. "The contest between the two doctors must thus properly turn not on the question whether persons and periods of Scottish Church history are correctly sketched and valued, but on the rights of the Church without a name, which the Dean uses as the standard of his criticisms. This Dr. Rainy fully perceives. . . ." But at the bottom, Stanley, just like the "Moderni" in Holland, seeks the essence of the Church in what is common to humanity, not in what is specifically Christian. We have no doubt that in those remarks Rauwenhoff has correctly stated the gist of the dispute. But we do doubt whether Dean Stanley is conscious of so fundamental a difference between himself and his antagonist. And it is worth noticing that the clearness with which Dr. Rainy recognises the character of the point in dispute is, in Rauwenhoff's eyes, a decided merit, while on the part of certain petulant critics on this side of the water, it has exposed him to unmerited reproach. . . . It is not without an æsthetic regret that he parts from a man like Dr. Rainy. He recognises and honours in him the glow of intense conviction, so powerful for the formation of churches and the fostering of a spirit of religion, which Moderatism with difficulty attains to. And so, though he feels it to be rather unfriendly in the Scottish Professor to ask where a position like the Dean's leaves room for a conviction strong enough for martyrdom, he regretfully confesses that the modern acknowledgment of the rights and importance of the finer shades of opinion, do make it difficult for a man to have many sharp convictions. He recognises the moral force of a Christianity that rests on positive conviction of supernatural truth, and though he cannot himself see how a scientific mind can hold such a position, freely admits that "the Church without a name" may learn from Dr. Rainy's lectures the need for a great deal of that which gave the old Church its great name. We confess to have read the article with much pleasure. It states the point in dispute with a fairness which has by no means been present in the strictures of certain Moderates of the new school in Scotland, who are themselves examples of the way in which "emancipation from dogma may proceed, under the form of party spirit"; and we are sure that no true-hearted adherent of a churchly Christianity of positive faith, will shrink from the test which Mr. Rauwenhoff proposes—the power of keeping hold of all classes of men.'

Here we must break off, thankful that our inadequacy is made up for by the kind co-operation of others. Dr. Rainy lived till the hour of perfect reconcilement, till the hour when misunderstandings even on earth were almost over. He has passed in a reverent hush, and we know what we have lost in him, the saint, the seer, the leader, the prophet, all subdued to an innocent and most wise gentleness. There will be no successor to him, and no successor is needed. The Church has her living Lord, and it is far better that her energies should be guided by the free and frank and democratic action of the rank and file. Men of special power will have special offices given to them, but for our own part we are most deeply convinced that our Nonconformist churches are most wisely guided by the judgment of the average man. Just as the world is wiser than any philosopher, so the Church is wiser than any Churchman. 'There is some one wiser than Voltaire and wiser than Napoleon : *c'est tout le monde.*' As Bagehot has said, popular judgment on popular matters may be crude and vague, but it is right. The long domination of the Free Church by Principal Rainy was so inevitable that it is quite useless to try to adjust the balance of its good and evil. If another Rainy is granted, then we shall see what will happen. In the meantime, with great calls sounding, with wide doors opening, with many adversaries waiting, she has to go forward a free, evangelical and spiritual Church of the Lord Jesus Christ.

January 3, 1907

IAN MACLAREN

We must be allowed to use the name which as we shall always be proud to remember first appeared in these columns. The last thing we ever dreamed of was writing an obituary notice of Dr. John Watson. It seems but the other day when he was with us in that abounding and rejoicing vitality which almost terrified those of a feebler make. So strong was the impression of this, that we did not at first give much weight to the telegrams in the papers. The blow fell suddenly, and in the turmoil of thought and feeling which it has evoked, we scarcely know how to write about him. We have been set the hard task of analysing and reproducing for others as a picture that which we feel most acutely as a reality. We have to do it at a time when we do not care, and are hardly able, to feel more than the reality. But certain features will remain as we continue to individualise and imagine him in the days that are to come. It is on these that we must dwell.

I

Now that we think of it, John Watson ever and anon gave expression to his Celtic presentiment of an early death. The past assumes a new significance. Three years before he retired, apparently in full vigour, and at a comparatively early age, he told his friends of his purpose. It was manifestly a deep purpose. He carried it through amidst all but universal remonstrance, without hesitation or misgiving. He looked backward to it without one single regret. His life, he would say, was not to be a long one, and perhaps he was not unpleased to see it passing. He contemplated, too early, the softer, fading aspects of our earthly life, the joy and rest and reunion of the world of hope. Those who looked at him while he was speaking could hardly take it all seriously. But he meant what he said. It is strange, too, that he died in America. To no Briton, perhaps, was America ever so dear as it was to him. He observed it, he admired it, he laughed at it, and he truly loved it. Indeed he seriously thought on his retirement that he would make his home in America, doing such occasional work as offered itself. Three times he had proved the place he held in American hearts, and now he has passed away among American friends. 'He was worn out,' he said when he retired, and we laughed at him, but we did not know what he knew.

It is on the loss of a friend that our thoughts are mostly lingering. Few men have been more beloved than John Watson. In the great city to which he gave his heart, in thousands of homes throughout the country, he will be lamented as one very near and very dear. Many of us know that the loss is beyond repair. No new friendship can make up for it. Dr. Watson had a watchful solicitude for those admitted to his inner circle. He never lost sight of them. He was always ready to succour and to comfort at the hours of need; he was ever doing kindnesses, and he appreciated and magnified the most trivial kindness to himself as very few men ever did. Of the desolation in his own household, where the air was always warm with love, we cannot speak.

His death is also an unspeakable loss to the Churches. When he resigned his charge, he really wished to be free. He believed that his years of indefatigable service gave him a right to freedom. But he very soon saw that he could not escape the yoke. The times needed him, and he recognised it. He was led to accept the Presidency of the Free Church Council, and we were all looking forward with great hope and thankfulness to the work he was to do for Nonconformity in England. By the retirement of his close friend, Dr. Oswald Dykes, the Principalship of Westminster College was vacant. Dr. Watson had done much to establish that institution, and when his name was brought forward as successor, he was reluctantly led to think it might be his duty to stand. There was no attraction of emolument. Another nominee with high claims had his warm regard, and he most unwillingly consented to come into competition with him. But then Dr. Watson passed a very humble judgment on his own qualifications for the position. He disparaged his learning, but he thought that he might be able to do something in bringing about a closer alliance between the College and the Churches, and in helping the Presbyterian Church of England to undertake more aggressive work among the masses. He would, we know, have been intensely relieved if the Church had preferred another. In the last long letter we received from him he said he had heard that an important Presbytery had voted against him and assumed that this was decisive. He expressed no regret, but a characteristic confidence that the interests of the College would not suffer in the hands of the eminent scholar preferred. We have little doubt, however, that the new sphere would have been open to him, and that he would have filled it most worthily. So we lost him, as it seems, when he was most precious to us. We saw in him a man who could speak to England, and when we most need such a man we must look for him no more. He had gathered his stores—his strength, his experience, his seriousness, his grasp of his own thoughts—and was ready to lead us into the new era, and then he was taken away. It is indeed a bitter loss—how bitter we shall realise through the days and years.

When we try to think of John Watson, it is on the unity, rather than on the diversity of his character that our thoughts soon settle. He was indeed on one side a man of the world, brilliant, witty, frank, engaging, affluent in conversation, the orator, the wit, the central figure. As a preacher and speaker, his eloquence, the nobleness and warmth of his tone, his keen sympathy, his percipiency put him in the foremost rank. But along with the exuberance and buoyancy, the freedom and the daring, there went a remarkable severity of self-discipline, a fixity of principle, a precision of thought and style, which made him a worthy ruler of men. We cannot distinguish between John Watson and Ian Maclaren. If our dear dead friend could speak to us at this moment, we know very well that he would urge us to write of him as first and last a Christian minister. His last words to us were that he stood on his twenty-five years in Liverpool—that his life-work had been done there. As a preacher he did not at once come to his own. In his early years he showed no ambition. He held a good place easily, and was a friend and associate of the best men, but few of his comrades imagined that he would become one of the personalities of the nation. In his early years his individuality was trammelled by his association with influential Conservative Presbyterians, and he was too true a man ever to abandon wholly the system that had moulded his youth. Indeed, he leaned much to it even to the end. But he found himself when he came to form a new congregation in Liverpool. There he came under new and strong influences. He gathered his own congregation by the most conscientious and unsparing labour, and the most brilliant ability. He built it up year by year till it was the largest and most influential in the city. It was on this rather than on his books that he loved to dwell. The reception of his books, indeed, gave him a natural and just joy, but he never made much of them in conversation. He would talk for ever on Sefton Park congregation, on the men who had helped him as office-bearers and members, and on the history of the people, rich and poor. From the first he had a high conception of pastoral duty, and to the end he contrived to visit every member of his congregation once a year. He bore a great affection to the city where he had been so long one of the purest and most potent influences. But his pulpit was his throne. At the close of his ministry, he claimed truly that he had preached Christ. The great thoughts of Incarnation and Atonement, which are the life and light of theology, always possessed him. His temper was truly catholic, and he was sensitive to changes, but he was evermore convinced that in the end theology reverts to its broad immemorial features and the New Testament language. He pressed home his message with personal force, that is, he had always in his mind, not merely ideas, but persons. He saw sin and pain not in the mass, but by their real tokens in the souls they bow down. The characters, the dangers, and the sorrows of his people were ever in his mind. Dr. Watson, as the nation knows, was a man of great oratorical power, but he never presumed on it. He studied hard for his sermons, and he had the power of ranging widely and fast without losing his point of view, or entangling himself in detail. Of all his religious convictions, the one to which he most constantly returned was that of the immortal hope. Since George Macdonald, there has been no such prophet of immortality. The vision always before his eyes was that of a heaven peopled with the crowding guests of God.

Dr. Watson strove very hard to present the Christian ideas in the forms of his own mind and age. At a certain period he seemed to discard at once outworn words and phrases. He wrote like a modern—as the fathers and even the schoolmen did in their day. This made him a close student of style. With Hazlitt, Pater, Stevenson, and above all with Lamb, he was very familiar. But his end was always practical. He was an artificer and master of phrases. But in our judgment he was at his best when he was stating truth in a calm, exact, measured way, and when he was making the concluding appeals of his sermons. His great conviction lifted a heavy load from many hearts that had been oppressed by the noise of conflict. He never treated any theme without a strong sense of moral responsibility for his hearers. He may have been at times imprudent and rash, but really great subjects subdued and restrained him. He found in them a call to recollection and to sober words. In the driving home of ethical truth there were very few to match him. No one more powerfully advocated the sanctity and beauty of the family tie, and no one more powerfully enforced the claims of citizenship. Though he very rarely spoke about the effect of his work, he never concealed his pride in the fact that many members of his congregation had taken a leading part in the government of Liverpool. He was, so far as we could judge, always at his best and always most at home in his own pulpit.

II

Many of our readers will recall the start of wonder and pleasure with which they read his first story in these columns. *Beside the Bonnie Brier Bush* had a reception which has not been paralleled in our time, and all his books, theological and general, have been very widely read. We cannot for our part draw a strict line between his fiction and his sermons. He was always preaching, and he attained his end perhaps as well in the informal as in the formal conveyance of his message. It is true to say that sentimentalism was alike his strength and his weakness, but those who imagined that John Watson was a weak sentimentalist were profoundly mistaken. His sentiment was very deep and true. He wrote himself once as a New Year's message: 'Be pitiful, for every man is fighting a hard battle,' and he lived up to it. We have never known any one whose life, if scrutinised, would show so many minute kindnesses, thoughtful attentions, unobtrusive consolations. All life seemed to present itself to him as simply an opportunity for doing kind things. But the man himself was, in every sense of the word, a strong man. He was the master of a deadly irony, and a withering sarcasm. Generally speaking, it was only in private conversation that he made use of these gifts. He looked upon them as wild beasts to be held in check. He was wont to say that the power of irony was a power which could never be employed to any good purpose by a Christian minister. To say that he never employed it in public would be an exaggeration, though we cannot recall an instance. He had often great provocation, and he knew well that he had the use of the weapon that would punish his assailant, but he deliberately kept silence. Few, if any, knew 'the weight of his terrible hand.' It would be unpardonable if we were to recall some of these characterisations which linger in the memory, for Dr. Watson regarded no man with bitterness. He could measure to a nicety, but he did not issue price-lists. He could be strong and severe, but he did not go out of his way to insult, to insinuate, or to sneer. He knew the darker aspect of Scottish life as well as most, for he had been familiar in his early days with the Bothy system; in fact, he long contemplated writing a Scots novel which would tell the worst, and when *The House with the Green Shutters* appeared, he remarked that he could have drawn the picture in darker lines. Dr. Watson had meditated very seriously and unshrinkingly on the objects and the real conditions of life, but something kept him back from saying all he thought and knew. He considered that there were in the world bitterness enough, sadness enough, pessimism enough, and so he bore the reproach of being a gushing sentimentalist very meekly, and made it his business to unlock and soften the hearts that had grown hard in prison.

In Dr. Watson the elements of Conservatism and Radicalism were strangely combined. By his upbringing he was Tory, and in fact he was by sympathy a Jacobite. Though connected with the Scottish Free Church, he inclined to favour Establishments, both in Scotland and in England. In general politics he was for the most part on the Conservative side, but he would never have made a good party man, for in many ways he was advanced in his views. Loving the order and stateliness of Anglican services, he utterly rejected sacerdotalism. He sympathised more and more as time went on with the Nonconformists in their struggle for a righteous settlement of the Education question. He was an Imperialist, but for the democratic institutions of America he had the warmest admiration. In some ways he was conventional. He loved ceremony and the innocent joys of life. He observed with keen interest the ways of the great, and his books brought him into contact with the highest, and even into royal circles. Academic pomp pleased him, but nothing could prevent him from seeing the humorous side, and pomposity in particular gave him the best opportunity for the exercise of his powers. He did not resent pomposity, but seemed rather to enjoy being patronised. But his friends will never forget the state of helpless laughter to which he brought them when describing his experiences. Dr. Watson never thought it any part of his duty to come forward in politics. His work, as he conceived it, was the work of the Christian ministry, and he came into the battle of public life only when he thought that great Christian and moral interests were concerned.

The temper of his life was eminently joyful, though, like every Celt, he had intervals of deep depression. With all his brightness he had borne his share of the burden of this unintelligible world, and could feel with those whom it oppressed. When we look back we can see better than before how he strove to encourage others, how he would not allow his occasional melancholy to cast a shadow, how he cultivated joy as the purely Christian temper of life. In any and every company he gave himself largely and freely. It did not matter who his companions were. The best that he could give them was at his disposal, and it was a strange exception, if any one ever met him, even casually, without being better and brighter for the meeting. Indeed, he gave away his life with prodigal generosity. His industry was constant; he lost no moment of time, and for years his activity might be described as restless and feverish. We have seen him often, after an exhausting day, go to bed in the early morning He would appear at breakfast as vivacious and blithe as if he had done nothing. The moment breakfast was over, he would take up his task and persevere with it till it was accomplished. Then he would go out to be the chief guest at a company which simply basked in his presence. He would pass from that to a round of visiting, then he would come in weary, and at dinner be the life and soul of the guests. He would go out from that to preach or lecture, and on his return he would carry on a conversation till two or three o'clock in the morning. This would go on for weeks at a time, varied only by the Sunday, and by incessant railway travelling. We grudge all this activity of the twentieth century, for it costs us many a cherished and thrice-prized life.

In his later years Dr. Watson gave much time to the study of Church history, and, like Lightfoot, he drew from it a message of cheer. He came to realise the life of the Divine Society. Christ, he perceived, had promised to be with His Church in the blaze of noon, in the dark, or in the twilight between the two, wherein mainly the course of her journey lies. He saw how the Church had seemed to perish, how her defenders had seemed to be confounded, and yet how truly the Lord's promise had been kept. He perceived—and would that he were with us to enforce the lesson in his own incomparable manner—how these alarms, and forebodings, and prophecies of dissolution that often shake the hearts of the faithful, drop into insignificance in the course of that vast history which has *not* fulfilled them.

May 9, 1907.

DR. BARNARDO[1]

It is more than thirty years since I first met Dr. Barnardo. He was addressing meetings in Inverness, and we were living in the same house. At that time he had begun to be famous, and was in the fullest vigour of his many-sided enthusiasm. We had endless talks at night, and I learned much from him. I conceived a strong belief in the man and a warm regard for him. This affection and admiration continued to the end. Communication with so busy a man in London is not easy, but we managed to maintain a measure of intercourse, and I was well able to see how his life developed. It was a life of continual growth, a life that never flinched, never wavered, a life which was spent to its last drop in the labour it loved. When Dr. Barnardo died, quite worn out, I was deeply touched to learn that he expressed his wish that I should have something to do with any memorial that might be written of him, and it is in obedience to his desire that these words are set down.

I

The great apparent characteristic of Dr. Barnardo was ardour. He flamed up into vehemence very

[1] Introduction contributed to the *Memoirs* of Dr. Barnardo by Mrs. Barnardo and James Marchant.

easily. Love, pity, wrath, scorn manifested themselves in turn almost volcanically. These bursts soon subsided, but very readily recurred. Dr. Barnardo was a man of strong opinions on many points. Latterly he became somewhat deaf and was wont to carry a fearful and wonderful instrument which he described as an ear trumpet. I never saw him use it for the purpose of hearing, but he employed it freely in thumping the back of his companion, whether to enforce the point of a joke or of an argument. He would run round the table pouring himself out, and then as his climax approached, he seized his ear-trumpet firmly. But one soon noticed that this great effervescence was not first or last among his qualities. He had that strange tenacity possessed by a few, to which it seems as if almost everything yields at last. Dr. Barnardo had taken up his work in life and he clung to it all the time. On general subjects he could talk very brightly. He was emphatically a gentleman, and there was a measure of justice, courtesy, and toleration in his speech which were somewhat surprising in a man so firm in his own mind. Matters of home interest to himself and his friends he would dwell upon with a genuine interest and sympathy but in the end he had only one subject. It was about the Homes and the children that he was always thinking, and when conversing on other themes one could sometimes see that 'his eyes were with his heart, and that was far away.' His shrewdness and humour came out plainly; he was a man who had one aim in life. In later years I came to know much of how he was regarded in his own Homes by his fellow-workers and the children. It is not too much to describe the feeling as that of affectionate reverence. He was a born leader if ever there was one, and his people followed him gladly. It is of supreme importance that the life of such a man should be written, if it be true, as F. W. H. Myers has said, that the record of a great and pure personality is the best bequest of time.

II

I am anxious to emphasise the fact that Dr. Barnardo was of the old school of philanthropists. Early in his days he was able to conceive the profound influence that may be given to one life. Dr. Barnardo started with hardly any advantages. All around him was difficult and even threatening, but he resolved to see what by God's help one man could do. He did not merely make speeches about the necessity of his work, nor did he show any great interest in Parliamentary reforms. He did the work—that was all. While others were talking and writing, he was pursuing his task of rescue. No one did more to effect the change that has come over our own nation in its view of the relative importance of political and social questions. No one did more to bring social problems to the front. But he himself was not an active politician. He would not, I am sure, have accepted the dictum that there is no obvious connection between politics and the good of society, but he would have refused to go to the other extreme. In a world of talkers Dr. Barnardo determined to do all he could for the miserable and the weak so long as he could, and that is the story of his life.

III

It must be noticed that he started and continued as a strongly convinced Evangelical believer. Religion was always uppermost with Dr. Barnardo. He accepted with the most childlike, simple, and absolute faith the gospel of the Cross. Is it not true that so far the greatest social reforms have been effected by men who hold the same views ? Dr. Barnardo was much influenced by the great Spurgeon, but it would be utterly misleading to range him in the usual way as a Churchman or a Nonconformist. I fancy he had little or no sympathy with the political aims of Nonconformity, and certainly he was a strong Protestant. He said, 'Grace be with all them that love our Lord Jesus Christ in sincerity.' Dr. Barnardo, like others of the old philanthropists, had no faith in utopias. He never ignored the great facts of life—sin and sorrow and death. All of us are under sentence of death, probably death by torture, and all of us have to fight the battle with temptations. Dr. Barnardo thought that when everything was done that could be done, much evil would remain. He did not believe that he had found Excalibur in the magic sword of democracy. He believed, however, with all his heart, that the sum of human misery could be indefinitely lessened and also that the gospel of the grace of Christ was a sword not wielded in vain. He himself preached continually and with extraordinary force and fervour. I have before me a sermon on the 'Cities of Refuge,' which he preached at the Metropolitan Tabernacle many years ago. It is remarkable for its red-hot earnestness. So far as I have heard Dr. Barnardo was invariably an evangelist. He lived, too, a hidden life of deep, prayerful, constant devotion, and without that he never could have carried his battle through.

IV

Dr. Barnardo gave to this service of the children what he had to give, and it was much. No one who really knew him could doubt that he was a man of great and commanding powers. If these powers had been exercised in the world of business, or in his own profession, they would certainly have brought him to the front. He had that very rare quality, the genius of organising. Sometimes at his meetings he would suddenly change his programme, to the discomfort of his associates, but generally it was found out that he had done the right thing. But what gave him his triumph was his unfeigned and passionate love for poor, oppressed, neglected children. This comes back to me as I think of him as by far the most striking feature of his character. It seemed as if he loved the mass and the individuals also, and it seemed as if his love had no limits. The children from whom others would turn away went straight into his heart as through an open door. He seemed to know every child of his multitude, or at least to know something of every one. He loved them and yearned over them as if they had been his own dear children. For nearly all his time I imagine that his working day was sixteen hours, and he seemed to hate the thought of a complete holiday. For his own family his affection was deep and tender, and particularly for his delicate child, whom he loved as John Bunyan loved his, but in the service of the outcast the full enjoyment of home life had to be largely sacrificed. Of course he was not perfect; he would have been the last to claim it. He made mistakes and suffered for them, but he was emphatically one of the few to whom the maxim can safely be applied that the man who never makes mistakes never makes anything.

V

It would be as far as possible from the truth to say that Dr. Barnardo missed his share of happiness. He had the fulfilment of that word of Christ, 'Whosoever will lose his life for My sake shall find it.' But measured by ordinary standards his life was a very hard one. This man was perhaps the best servant of the empire, but no recognition, no honours came to him. The small salary he received was hardly enough to supply his necessities. His work was incredibly wearing, and accompanied by infinite worries. He was always in need of money for his ever extending enterprises, and it had to be raised largely through his effort. Dr. Barnardo was a proud and sensitive man, but for the sake of the children he humbled himself to beg. He had experience of the somewhat bitter saying of Lord Shaftesbury, that the British people have an immense capacity for enthusiasm, and an equal incapacity for giving money. The worries he encountered would have goaded most people to madness, and it is idle to deny that they told upon him and shortened his life. But he never thought of giving up; he held on in the darkest hours to his task.

In addition, Dr. Barnardo had much obloquy to face. I will not say that he met the terrible resistance which the early philanthropists had to face. He did not suffer as the anti-slavery men, as the men who attacked the hanging laws, and as Lord Shaftesbury did in his campaign for the factory hands. But there is perhaps no hostility so violent and reckless as that roused by the exposure of brutality, cruelty, and filth by which money is made. So Dr. Barnardo had his full share of violent abuse. But he was of the same breed as the philanthropists who in their struggle faced lives of insult and long-continued poverty and shameful and violent death. Lord Shaftesbury was habitually despondent, but

Dr. Barnardo had a high and buoyant courage, and his sufferings seemed to anneal him like fire. The strengthenings he had acquired so painfully helped him when he was down in the thick of the fight, and he did far more to convert public opinion than he himself knew. Then his expectations were measured, He was not of those who believe that nothing but stupidity prevents universal happiness. He was one of those who recognised that when every other obstacle to progress has been removed, human nature will stand right across the road and that only Christ can deal with it. Never even amidst his gleams of success did Dr. Barnardo expect a world at ease. Each day he rose to face the storm. He had many solaces. He had his home. He drew to him the love and help and confidence of many among the leading men and women of his time. What he valued still more was the affection of the children, and if the mystical saying is true, that all love is returned, he must have had much of that. Anyhow he never complained and he never boasted. He belonged to the small transfigured band whose reward is with them and their work before them.

VI

Many who loved him were moved to tears at the tributes rendered him after his death. The gracious messages of the King and Queen, the noble leading article in *The Times*, Mr. Owen Seaman's verses in *Punch*—these and many other things showed that the world had not been so blind to the greatness of his achievement as he himself supposed. It was instinctively felt, even among those who had reviled him, that a man who had done the work of reclamation on so great a scale was on a different level of nobility, independence, and clear-sightedness from the mass of his generation. Dr. Barnardo had entered into the mind of Christ by his practical service more deeply than almost any other, and men knew it. There must be few indeed who have done the work given them more diligently, more bravely, or with a more simple heart.

1907.

PRINCIPAL HUTTON

The Rev. Dr. Hutton, of Paisley, so long known as the indomitable and fearless champion of Disestablishment, died quite suddenly on Friday. He had been attending the meetings of the General Assembly of the United Free Church, and taking a very active part in the discussions on Disestablishment. The old man (he had nearly attained his eighty-third year) was much exhausted, and the end seems to have been merely the result of age.

Dr. Hutton was, we repeat, indomitable. It does not appear that he ever thought of retirement either from his pastoral duties or his public work. Most men come to seek for a quiet backwater in the river of life, where the pressure of the current can no longer reach them. But Dr. Hutton was not one of these. He had to know by experience that 'living is outliving.' But he did not outlive his interests. He fell upon the field of battle, and on all sides he has been recognised as one whom no foe ever made afraid, no victory ever rendered insolent, and no defeat ever irritated or depressed. It is most honourable to the Church of Scotland and a most gratifying sign of the times that in the General Assembly and from the leading pulpits of that body warm and tender tributes have been paid to the great fighter against privilege. As was written about his comrade, Henry Renton of Kelso :—

> 'A death like thine hath called a truce,
> Heard round about thee many a mile,
> And men forget their daily use
> To stand beside thy grave awhile.
>
> 'To pay that honour due to one
> Who bore the battle brunt of life,
> And ranked a second unto none
> Where conscience called him to the strife.'

Dr. Hutton has been followed to his grave by the universal respect and regret of his countrymen.

His life-work was done in one pastorate—in the church at Paisley, of which he became minister in 1851. We have been told years ago of the spiritual warmth in Dr. Hutton's congregation, of the numbers of young men who waited on his ministrations, of the depth, force, and distinction of his sermons. His literary abilities were unquestionably of a high order. There was that blending of the new with the old in his style which always rouses interest, and on occasion, as in his tribute to Dr. Rainy, he rose to a high and solemn strain of eloquence. He was also remarkably acute, quick to detect fallacies, and a master of pungent phrases and sentences. But to the general public he was known mainly as the advocate of religious equality, and with this he was content. Some of his most intimate friends rather resented this. They said that Hutton might have revealed himself far more truly and fully if he had not been everywhere expected to speak on one subject. The same thing was said about Edward Miall. Miall had literary gifts which might have given him a high place among the graceful, thoughtful, and pensive essayists of his time. He had a truly poetic and tender sense of the encompassing darkness of life. But he saw it to be his duty to concentrate himself on one cause, and so did Dr. Hutton. In Dr. Hutton's mind the cause of temperance was hardly second, if at all second, to that of Disestablishment.

We have seen him called a statesman, and it is true that he took much part in political warfare, and had a strong influence over Liberal politicians. But in the ordinary sense of the word he was not a statesman, at least if we take Henry Vaughan's definition of the statesman :—

> 'The darksome statesman hung with weight and woe,
> Like to thick midnight fog moved there so slow,
> He did not stay, nor go.'

Dr. Hutton had nothing of the opportunist about him. He appeared insensible to considerations of prudence and policy. He pressed in all circumstances the interests of the cause which so strongly held him. So far as we are aware, he was no organiser. No movement ever known to us was so little organised or so badly organised as the cause of religious equality in Scotland. Dr. Hutton did not even seek to enlist the young and rising men of his Church. Nor did he do much in the way of appealing to the public through the press, though he wrote frequently and trenchantly in the newspapers and elsewhere. His service was rendered in speech and in debate, and it was a great, weighty, and influential service. In all his speeches that we ever read or heard, there was strong logical argument. But he could dot the dark expanse of heather with tufts of flowers. He could be very playful and very amusing. No matter what the temptation was, Dr. Hutton never descended to vulgar violence. His weapon was the keen and glittering sword; he did not fight with his fists. He had no diplomacy and no art, but he believed, and therefore spoke. The Church that knew him best did not mistake the man. When Principal Cairns died, Dr. Hutton received the highest distinction that could have been conferred upon him; he was appointed Principal of the Theological College. A Voluntary so strong and pronounced naturally did not desire union with churches whose position was indefinite or adverse. Thus the negotiations for union between the United Presbyterian Church and the Free Church, alike in their earlier stage and in their later, did not command his sympathy. Latterly, indeed, he saw that union was inevitable, but he held that the union of 1900 was ten years too soon. However, he went in with it; and it was characteristic of the man that when the great testing trouble came there was none more loyal, none more ardent, none more fearless in the fight for the despoiled and harassed Church than the Principal.

Dr. Hutton was in truth a faithful son of the old Secession Church. He had drunk deeply of the teaching on the relation of Church and State delivered by the fathers. The dust has gathered thick on the many sermons, pamphlets, and books which the Voluntary controversy called forth. We are not sure that even Dr. Taylor Innes could claim to know them all. Certainly our own knowledge is superficial enough, and yet a very slight knowledge is sufficient to show that no more powerful and searching treatment of the difficult problems involved in the relations between Church and State is to be found anywhere than in some of these productions. What can be better than the calm, masterly, and truly Christian work of Lawson on *The Power of the Civil Magistrate in Matters of Religion*? Who are more trenchant and logical than Marshall of Kirkintilloch and Coventry Dick? There are others, but it must suffice to name these. We ought not, however, to forget Dr. Young of Perth, the minister under whom Hutton was brought up. Dr. Young was a thorough Voluntary, and no doubt did much to impress the ardent mind of his pupil. The argument for Disestablishment which appeals to most is that once stated very powerfully in the Free Assembly by Dr. Robertson Smith, that the new ethical conception of the State forbids the State to give secular privileges and emoluments to any one denomination. All this is carried in the phrase religious equality. Dr. Hutton stood for religious equality, but what moved him and men of his school far more strongly was the religious consideration. They held that Disestablishment was needed not so much to right Dissenters as to right Christianity. Establishment dimmed the true glory of the Gospel Church. They conceived that the union between Church and State was essentially contrary to the first principles of Christianity, and always and everywhere injurious. It was as a Christian man believing in the Lord Jesus Christ as the Head of the Church that Hutton pleaded. He would have said that the Christian religion originally made its way in the world, not only without the patronage of the secular authorities, but in defiance of their enmity and power. He would have considered it inconsistent with piety, with faith, and with reason 'to suppose that the Divine author of Christianity should suffer that one thing, which is transcendently the best on earth and the object of His peculiar care, to depend for its effective existence on arrangements in the political constitution of a nation.' It was not the sense of injustice, galling as that sometimes is, that urged him on to his life battle. It was the conviction that the Church of Christ cannot do her best work in alliance with the State, and that the tutelage of the State is always hampering and often fatal to spiritual power and growth.

It is not surprising that under these circumstances Dr. Hutton should have looked very coldly on proposals for co-operation and conference with the Established Church. In this we are not able to sympathise with him. We believe there is a drawing together of Christian men in all the churches, and that the end of it will be the establishment of justice and the peace that results therefrom. It has been questioned whether the cause of Disestablishment has made progress in the last thirty years; and no doubt, so far as politics go, it has been subjected to many thwartings and bafflings. Yet, in spite of all this, we are firmly convinced that it has made a real and great advance, and that it is increasingly engaging the sympathies of thoughtful and Christian men everywhere. The catholic-minded Dean Alford, in one of the last things he ever wrote, pointed out that we encounter our greatest trouble, not in the matter of deeds, but of words. 'Words, like weapons, are soon whetted to keenness when war is in the air. The most important steps toward our great end will be drawn on one after another by the deep working of Christian public opinion; in other words, by the wisdom of God's Spirit. They will come in the train of other and unsuspected designs; they will not be recognised as of great import till they have passed by. Many a deed is done, many a word is spoken which not a soul on earth contemplated an hour before, but which, when done or spoken, shifts the level of human thought and opens a new era for mankind.' Yes, the spirit of truth and justice is opening up the way. The barriers are falling. The spirit of intolerance, of disdain, of superiority, of exclusiveness is vanishing. It is vanishing in spite of the fact that it never had more resolute and bitter champions. They fight every concession, and yet in the end the conflict is settled against them, and measures are passed by an irresistible drift of national conviction. There have been reactions, and there will be reactions again. All the same, the trend and the end are sure. All things make for righteousness, and the slow pace at which our way has been fought hitherto is already so much accelerated that we may expect in the comparatively near future, and not through revolutionary violence, measures of which the most sanguine once hardly dared to dream. Towards this the labours and sacrifices of men like Dr. Hutton have contributed much. It is due to him and others like him that we are able to believe that there never was a time when the soldiers and servants of religious justice had more reason to thank God and take courage.

June 4, 1908.

PRINCIPAL MARCUS DODS

THE long illness of Dr. Marcus Dods came to its close early on Monday morning. He has been almost utterly helpless and often in great pain through many months. He has had weary days and nights of suffering. Until lately he has been able to read a little and to talk for a short time in the day with much of his old vivacity and spirit. He was affectionate and brave and hopeful. But it was only too plain that he could never recover. In answer to a congratulation on his appointment to the Principalship of the New College, he said, 'It has come too late.' He loved life, and he seemed to love his work more than ever, and he had dreams of what he might do for his College. But since the day when he recognised that he was moving towards death he has humbly accepted the will of God, and he passed from us in full assurance of the life to come, though little able to conceive its manner and way.

It is impossible for me to write anything like an estimate of Dr. Dods. He was the best friend and the most Christlike man I have ever known. He was in his daily work and conversation a living evidence of Christianity. There were many who have never lost their joyful confidence in Christ, and they owe this to him as much as to any.

In the circumstances I ask to be pardoned if I seem to dwell unduly on my own relations with Dr. Dods. They have been constant for nearly thirty years, ever since the time when I induced him to put in print some of his expository lectures. He was a contributor to the first number of *The British Weekly*, and to almost every number until his last sickness came upon him. Much of what he wrote was unsigned, but much was signed. But the relations between us were not merely business relations. I might perhaps say that they were relations of great intimacy, whereby I had the unspeakable privilege of knowing him as one man may seldom know another.

The outstanding thought that comes to me in this hour of deprivation is the thought of his grand character. Years ago we were sitting side by side in the memorable Free Church Assembly debate which ended in the removal of Dr. Robertson Smith from his chair. On that occasion Dr. Begg made a characteristic speech on the conservative side. Dr. Dods turned to me and said: 'He is a grand natural man.' He himself spoke in defence of Smith in a really noble utterance. Dr. Rainy, the leader of the other side, said that it was the finest thing he had ever heard. Dr. Dods began with a natural greatness of soul. If it can truly be said of any one that he is naturally Christian, then it could be said of Dr. Dods. But he was a Christian in the full sense of the word, and all that was pure and high in him was reinforced by faith, by prayer, by the practice of the presence of God, by the imitation of Christ.

There was something wonderful in his kindness. He did not go out of his way for occasions of self-sacrifice. He found them to his hand, and took them up one by one. During a trying year of life, when I was searching for health with not too much hope of finding it, Dr. Dods, then a busy minister in Glasgow, found time to write me every Monday a long letter of several quarto pages, in which he included every bit of news and comment that he could think of in order to interest and cheer me. I had no claim on him; many at that time knew him far better. If he did this for me, what must he have done for others? But if he had only done this for me I should have cherished his memory with everlasting gratitude.

So kind was he that it was a positive pain for him to refuse any request, even though the granting of the request might inconvenience him. He could not be forced to publish what he did not think fit to publish, but he was always ready to oblige even at the cost of time which could not well be spared. He loved books, and he liked to review them. But his happiest time was when he found a book which he could enthusiastically praise. I remember well his delight in Principal Edwards's Commentary on First Corinthians. Within a day or two after I sent him a copy, he wrote me in terms of rapture. They used to say that he was too enthusiastic in his praises, but when any one told him that he merely smiled. I could mention not a few books which were helped into large circulations by his early and warm eulogy. His taste was most catholic; he laid stress upon the excellence of workmanship and intent, and easily overlooked differences of opinion, and even grave differences.

Another characteristic in which Dr. Dods excelled all other men known to me was his magnanimity. 'He nothing common did or mean.' He always put the best interpretation on anything that happened. If one of his letters did not at once find an answer, he assumed that there was some reason for the delay. If the publication of any of his articles was delayed he never made any trouble, but assumed the postponement to be matter of necessity. If any one wrote or spoke against him he might flare up for the moment at the injustice, but would soon find an excuse, and was only too ready to suppose that the misunderstanding was his own fault. There was a generous incredulity at his heart. He was slow to wrath, and especially very slow to believe anything against those whom he cared for. He was not only willing but even anxious to hear the other side in every controversy, even when his own mind had been resolutely made up. 'Wait till you are seventy,' he would say with that unforgettable smile.

Then he was the very soul of veracity. It was disagreeable for him to criticise unfavourably. I scarcely remember any slashing review from his pen. When he did not approve he preferred to be silent. When he encouraged and praised he meant all that he said. There was something emphatically true about all his work and life. His days were laid out in regular order, and he did not allow the distraction of newspapers or visitors till the back of his work was broken. Morning by morning he was at his desk with his blue sheet of paper before him, and his pen in his hand. By the time the morning was over much had usually been accomplished. A few weeks ago when I last saw him he told me how he had loved to write; the exercise of the pen was a pleasure to him. He would review almost any book, and his reviews were invariably competent, interesting, and careful. He never made a mistake that I know of in matters of fact. Those who challenged his accuracy had reason to regret their temerity. His strong, bold, beautiful handwriting was a delight to the printers. He was punctual and trustworthy to the uttermost. One could depend on getting his manuscript on or before the hour when it was promised. If he was impatient of anything it was of disorderly and slovenly work. His hours were so well laid out and so filled with work that hardly any life of our time can have been more fruitful.

He was singularly bold in his way of speech, even when he knew that what he said would provoke opposition. At the Pan-Presbyterian Council in London long ago I heard him deliver a paper in which he spoke of the 'errors and immoralities' in the Old Testament. When the meeting was over we spent some hours together, and I ventured to ask him whether he thought the words were quite justified. He replied gravely that he had considered the matter. Afterwards Professor A. B. Davidson took exception in conversation to both words. He said he would admit that there was religious idealisation in the Old Testament, and that morality was progressive, but that what was immoral now was not necessarily immoral then. This opens a great controversy, but I give the incident as characteristic of the two men. Dr. Davidson was not a whit less truthful than Dr. Dods, but his habit of mind was more hesitating. In any case you always knew that Dr. Dods told you frankly all that was in his mind. He was not keeping back any secret unbelief. He was grandly and frankly and constantly truthful.

But to say this is to say little. Dr. Dods was in his daily walk and conversation a living evidence of Christianity. In one of the last articles he contributed to *The British Weekly*—it was on his favourite subject of St. Augustine's *Confessions*—he said that St. Augustine was one of the few who really loved God. Dr. Dods was another. 'I am the Almighty God; walk before Me and be perfect,' was an injunction ever in his mind. He was a friend of God. If there was something very simple and homely in his religion, there was that also which was august and profound. His devotion was not ecstatic or ostentatious. It was recollected, concentrated, tranquil. I do not think he was much at home in revival meetings, but religion was the great and ruling element in his life, and no one could have much intercourse with him without perceiving it.

Of Dr. Dods's noted ability and scholarship and of his power as a preacher I shall leave others to write. He was always visibly a great man under whatever aspect you might see him. For many years he did me the signal honour of carrying on a weekly exchange of letters, which were for the most part letters of friendship. I cannot adequately describe the effect of those letters. Their wisdom, their humour, their patient considerateness, their far-sightedness, their frankness came as an ever fresh surprise. But perhaps it was in a long conversation that Dr. Dods showed at his very best, and that you saw fully the hid treasures of his nature—his strength, his courage, his charm. In early days he was assistant librarian to the Signet Library in Edinburgh. This laid the foundation of his vast knowledge of books, a knowledge so great that I have only once or twice known it exceeded. But he was a scholar as distinct from a bookman. He was willing to read almost anything, but he carefully sifted his library, and he studied the enduring books. In this way his mind was nobly built up. On the strange fortunes and destinies of the Christian Church he looked with interest and hope. He came to be very happy in teaching students, but he did not seek a professorship, and would have been glad to remain in the pulpit. 'There is something about preaching that keeps life sweet,' he used to say.

Dr. Dods was in fact unconscious of his own greatness. He was the humblest of men, and he never offered counsel unless it was asked for. But unconsciously he had a haunting influence on those who knew him. Unconsciously he prompted them to do right. His ideals were very high, and though most forgiving he never came to terms with frailty, or consented to take a low view of what man by God's grace may be. The memory of him is at once a stimulus and a reproach. He demeaned himself so nobly in the critical and testing occasions of his life, he had such refinements of loyalty, such wonderful secrets of patience and endurance, that one could not fail to be moved and humbled, if nothing more, by intercourse with him. I have no hope of making up his loss or of finding such another friend again. But when we see not our tokens, and when the voices that helped and cheered fall silent one by one, we think of what has been and of what yet may be.

April 29, 1909.

DR. ALEXANDER M'LAREN

Dr. M'Laren passed in peace on Thursday in the fulness of years and honours. He died in Edinburgh, where he had many friends. He loved to talk of his first visit to that city, the rapture with which he beheld it, and of the thoughts which its beauty and its history stirred in his young mind. He remembered also hearing the great Dr. Chalmers talking like a tender father to a company of poor people. For days before his death he had been withdrawn from the loving watchers at his side. All the air was held in a solemn stillness. Till close on the end he had worked at his lifelong task as a Servant and Teacher of the Word of God. He had very nearly completed his great series of Expositions. There was no failing, no decay. What he wrote last is as fresh and strong as any work of his prime. For the present, at least, we shall attempt no biography. The outward events of his life are few. He spent his life as a Baptist minister for nearly twelve years at Southampton, and afterwards at Manchester. His career has an immense stretch—over the extraordinary period of nearly sixty-five years. But we give one letter, only part of which has hitherto been published.

It was agreed that it should be printed in full after his death.

CARR BRIDGE, N.B.,
September 1, 1905.

MY DEAR NICOLL,—I suppose that you are back at work again, and so I wish a word with you as to this month's *British Monthly.* I am very much obliged to you for planning and to your contributor for executing it, and I hope the readers will allow for kindly exaggeration, which makes me rather ashamed. If I had known of the intention to publish, I should have craved an opportunity of supplying material to fill two regrettable gaps. I do not know whether you can do anything still to fill them up, but I should be grateful if it could be done somehow.

The first of them touches on sacred matter, in regard to which I am habitually reticent, as I should and must be, but which should have a foremost place in any notice of me. I refer to my married life. My wife, Marion M'Laren, was my cousin. We were much together from our earliest days. Her father, James M'Laren, was an Edinburgh citizen of high standing, a deacon for many years in Dr. Lindsay Alexander's church, and a compeer of worthies like Adam Black, Charles Cowan, George Harvey, and other strong men of their day. The atmosphere of his house was redolent of the best traditions of Scottish religion and culture, a home of plain living and high thinking. With all its large and happy group of children I was as a brother, and the childish bonds grew stronger and graver as the children grew to be men and women, and they are stronger than ever to-day between the few survivors and myself. In 1856 Marion M'Laren became my wife. God allowed us to be together till the dark December of 1884. Others could speak of her charm, her beauty, her gifts and goodness. Most of what she was to me is for ever locked in my heart. But I would fain that, in any notices of what I am, or have been able to do, it should be told that the best part of it all came and comes from her. We read and thought together, and her clear, bright intellect illumined obscurities and "rejoiced in the truth." We worked and bore together, and her courage and deftness made toil easy and charmed away difficulties. She lived a life of nobleness, of strenuous effort, of aspiration, of sympathy, self-forgetfulness, and love. She was my guide, my inspirer, my corrector, my reward. Of all human formative influences on my character and life hers is the strongest and the best. To write of me and not to name her is to present a fragment.

'I should also have wished to have had the name of the Rev. David Russell, Congregational minister, of Glasgow, mentioned. To him, under God, I owe the quickening of early religious impressions into living faith and surrender, and to him I owe also much wise and affectionate counsel in my boyish years. He became my brother-in-law at a later period, and during all his long and honoured ministry he was my friend. I deeply revere his memory. I know, as few did, his patient work, his quaint freshness of thought and speech, his simplicity of life and steadfastness in cleaving to duty, his profound devoutness and his large heart, and I should have liked to have had my great obligations to him set prominently forth.

'I do not know if you can do anything, nor what you can do, to gratify my wishes in these respects, but I tell you what they are, and am sure that you will help me, if you see any way to do so.—Yours affectionately,

'ALEX. M'LAREN.

'*De profundis amavit.*'

I

We think first of his gifts and graces, then of his discipline of these, and then of his lifelong and almost fierce concentration on his work as a Baptist minister.

His natural gifts were extraordinary. He was out of sight the most brilliant man all round we ever knew. From his youth he looked like a Highland chieftain born to command. In any company where he sat was the head of the table. Before you knew he was a prophet you were sure he was a king. Who can forget that wonderful face, tender and stern, more beautiful and more saintly as the years went on, with the lights and shadows sweeping over it? Who can forget the flash of those magnetic, dominating eyes? There was a kind of regal effulgence about him in his great moments. He might have been anything—soldier, politician, man of letters, man of science, and in any profession he would have taken the head. He was gifted with a swift and clear-cutting intellect. He had also a true vein of poetry and genius. He could master any subject, and he had an all-sided strength and capacity. These gifts were early brought into captivity to the obedience of Christ. If ever any one was apprehended of Christ Jesus in early years, it was Alexander M'Laren. The religious training of his youth, which he loved to describe, seized him, held him, ruled him through all his many years. Never was any one more profoundly loyal to the lessons of the morning. He desired no other and no better thing than that the end of his life should circle round the beginning, only with a deeper conviction and a stronger love at last.

We shrink from writing about his religious life,

but it was hid with Christ in God. Those who observed him recognised that he drank from fountains older than the world, and for him they were always running fresh. In his later years it seemed to be his supreme desire to obtain a fuller communion with God in Christ. Although not mystical in his writings, he loved the mystics, and pondered over the sermons of Tauler and such books with a wistful eagerness. He knew by experience, as the true mystics knew, that God is the Rewarder of them that diligently seek Him. He proved the truth of that word. He was continually alive to the great realities of sin and grace, and this was the secret of the intense and solemn emotion that burned into the midst of heaven when he spoke to the people. Though he was very chary of speaking on such themes, I think he had some belief in the actual communion of the living with the dead, and he sometimes touched on it when his memory recurred to old dark hours. But in public his sole business was to expound the Word of God.

II

As wonderful as his gifts was the use he made of them. They were all disciplined for one purpose. He toiled terribly that he might be an effective preacher. He made himself a scholar familiar with Greek and Latin, and with the best in literature, English and Continental. With great labour he mastered and perfected a style. Carlyle was a potent influence in his early years. Browning he much preferred to Tennyson, though he had much of Tennyson's finish and music. Still there were traces of Carlyle and of Browning in his work at times, and more in his talk—something of brusqueness, something of fierceness, something of cutting through to the heart of things. But his fastidious taste was always in exercise. He made much of style in judging the merits of authors, and he thought that among living prose writers Joseph Conrad was the best.

Above all, he taught himself to speak in that style. Thomas Binney touched him powerfully in his early years. He resolved that he would not read sermons, but speak them, and that the spoken sermon should be as careful and as polished as the written sermon. He used to say that it took him years to accomplish this, and I can well believe it, for the result was miraculous. I have had in my hands some five thousand of the notes of his sermons, and I think I can say positively that the finest sentences were not found in the notes. They say that in the early years of his ministry he would pause a long time for a word. This never took place when I heard him, but he had learned his lesson. He had the temperament of an orator, and he acquired the rare faculty of speaking better English than he could write. It was amazing to see him in the pulpit, absorbed by the passion of the moment, and yet summoning and dismissing his phrases. You could see the double process going on, the mind shaping the consummate sentence behind the act and ardour of utterance. At last words came at his call, or without being called. He commanded words as an emperor *and* as a magician. In his very loftiest flights one hardly knew whether he spoke or sang; it was ‘Speech half asleep or song half awake.’

Every detail of the service was attended to in the same manner—the prayer, the Bible reading, the choice of hymns. He could not have been slovenly if he had tried to be. The last time I heard him speak was at the jubilee meeting of the Rev. Arthur Mursell, of which he was chairman. What a speech! The superb finish, the ease and grace that marked it were unforgettable. No living man could have come within measurable distance of it, and yet all was effortless.

III

All these disciplined gifts and graces were concentrated on his work as a minister—one might say as a Baptist minister.

A phrase much in his mouth was ‘this ministry,’ and another phrase was ‘neither priest nor philosopher, but messenger and proclaimer.’ He knew philosophy, and he knew how philosophies came and went. ‘The feet of them that are to carry thee out also are already at the door.’ To him preaching was the exposition of the eternal divine thought. Anything else was not preaching. So the Bible was his book. Through his long life he was continually studying it in Hebrew and in Greek. Like Dale, in his latter days he put Westcott's Commentaries above all the rest. Nothing interested him more in recent years than Dr. Moulton's New Testament Grammar, and the translation of the New Testament as affected by the discovery of the Greek papyri. All the wisdom of the world was to him contained in the Bible, but his business was to apply the Bible to life, and he read very widely in general literature. For biographies and sermons he cared nothing, but he knew the best novels well. The Waverley Novels he knew so intimately that latterly he could not read them. But Dumas continued to be a great favourite, especially the memorable series which includes the *Vicomte de Bragelonne.* Books of travel attracted him. He was a close student of history, and not ignorant of science. He studied the living book of humanity. His whole effort was to bring Bible truth into effective contact with the human heart.

Every one knows his method of preaching. His people, as one of his friends said, 'were fed with the three-pronged fork.' He had an extraordinary gift of analysing a text. He touched it with a silver hammer, and it immediately broke up into natural and memorable divisions, so comprehensive and so clear that it seemed wonderful that the text should have been handled in any other way. He sought to give truth an edge; he brought everything to a point. His style in his early Manchester sermons was richer and more adorned than in his later. His desire to get at men's souls simplified his speech. He proved himself more than adequate in the profoundest parts of Scripture, and I do not think he ever rose higher than in his exposition of the Epistle to the Colossians, where he expounds the cosmic significance of Christ. His spirit yoked itself with the loftiest thoughts and imaginings of prophets and apostles.

This concentration involved great sacrifices. Dr. M'Laren conceived it his duty to preach certainties, and only certainties. In the main he was what is called orthodox, but on the subject of eternal punishment he believed that the New Testament gave no clear teaching, some passages pointing to universal punishment, and others to universal restoration. But I do not remember that he ever stated this view in any sermon. He preferred to dwell on the certainty of sin's punishment. There were many who thought that he might have done much as a mediator between Church and modern thought. They considered that he, above all others, was the man who should lead his brethren with a clear lamp held patiently aloft, and throwing its light so broadly on their steps that when they came up with him they could not believe they had ever doubted of the way. But he deliberately declined the task, though not unwilling in conversation to state his views upon vexed problems.

For the same reason he rarely and reluctantly intervened in public affairs. When he did, his speeches were remarkable for their wisdom and fire. But they were few. He would say that he worked upon a very small reserve of force, but I believe that he could not bear to be away from the true work of his life—the exposition of triumphant certainties.

Nor was he a constructive, dogmatic theologian. He believed that if he explained the New Testament as it stood, the truth would go home. So he did little or nothing to restate, for example, the doctrines of the Incarnation and the Atonement. He held on his way in his own quiet course. I suppose he was like the man who, when asked to expound what God is, replied : 'I know if I am not asked.' It is hardly needful to say that he never took subjects of the day into his pulpit. He might preach a funeral sermon or make a reference to some impressive public event, but he did so very rarely. His sermons were, to use a favourite word of Mr. Howells, aoristic, or we may call them timeless. They had hardly any direct relation to the circumstances of the hour.

I have thought sometimes that he concentrated himself not merely on the ministry, but on the Baptist ministry. He seemed to have none of the ordinary ambitions of a preacher. He went to a very small congregation on a very small salary, and remained for the best years of his youth, in spite of all invitations to remove. When he came to Manchester there was only a moderate congregation in a moderately sized chapel to receive him. He created his own place by the sheer power of his preaching. People had to come to him; he did not go to them. Such was his attractive power that he ministered to one of the greatest and most influential congregations in Manchester. But he did not bow his proud head one inch to win any hearing. He was exceedingly unwilling to preach outside of the Baptist denomination. For example, he had no more ardent admirers than the Presbyterians of Scotland, but very few of them ever had the opportunity of listening to him. It was most difficult to induce him to preach any special sermon. So far was he from seeking to be included in programmes, that secretaries had to go on their knees almost in order to get his name. In fact, he seemed to prefer the humblest place. For village chapels he had a great love, and many of his finest utterances would be given in some poor House of Christ crowded by a rustic audience. Amidst the modern developments of church life he harked back to simple and primitive ways, the ways of the Quakers, the ways of the Pen Folk. He had to yield to the current of his time, and he did so with full conviction. But statistics, organisation, machinery, crowds, elaborate music, display, advertising—these things were not to his taste. We have said that he might have done great things in literature, but he would not be enticed away. He did speak at times about writing a volume of Scottish Baptist idylls, but he played smilingly with the idea, as Robert Browning did with the idea of his writing a novel on Napoleon. It never came to anything beyond a few pages. He translated for his own pleasure a good many letters of Luther in a most original and graphic style, but he would not go on with them. Once he very nearly accepted a professorship in Regent's Park College, but it was coupled with an engagement to preach in Bloomsbury Chapel every Sunday morning. Also, when very ill and deeply depressed by the death of his wife, he wrote to a publisher friend, suggesting that he should do literary work. But these were only passing moods. He was a minister of the Word, a minister among the Baptists, faithful to the death, working in the inspiration of the early days to which his heart held firm.

In this way he refused almost everything. He was always saying no. Every visitor whom he suspected of a new proposal was received at first with a certain gruffness and suspicion, soon disarmed into smiling gentleness. His first book of sermons was simply dragged out of him. It was printed from reporter's notes, and he was got to agree to a private publication. Then he had to give it to the public, and others followed. But if he had been left to himself he would never have published any sermons. I take pride in having suggested to him the preparation of his Expositions of Holy Scripture, which have been so widely read in this country, in the Colonies, and in America. I cannot say that he received the suggestion too graciously, but in the end I believe it gave him much pleasure to be working to the last, and the later volumes contain much more new matter than the earlier volumes did.

I have said nothing of his wit, his humour, his sarcasm, his sympathy. I have said nothing of the white light he threw upon men and movements. I have said nothing of the aloofness which, until his release from ministerial duty, prevented him from cultivating intimate friendships with men of his own intellectual rank. He had a hearty love for Lancashire, and especially for the character of the Lancashire people, on which he would dwell with great delight and many amusing stories. He was gratified by the recognition which he received from the University of Manchester, and took pleasure in his work as a Governor of Rylands' Library. But I think there can be very few cases where a man of his noble and magnificent powers had so limited a range of intercourse with the more potent personalities of his time. This was his own choice, his own sacrifice.

> 'We pass; the path that each man trod
> Is dim or will be dim with weeds.'

But it is difficult to believe that Dr. M'Laren will be soon forgotten. It is difficult to believe that his Expositions of the Bible will be superseded. Will there ever again be such a combination of spiritual insight, of scholarship, of passion, of style, of keen intellectual power? He was clearly a man of genius, and men of genius are very rare. So long as preachers care to teach from the Scriptures they will find their best help and guide in him. That remains, but we who knew him know what has been taken from us as we recall the man, his heart, his voice, his mien, his accent, his accost. We shall not see his like again. We know also that in him as much power was kept back as was brought out. He did his work not merely for the time, but for the time to come. He spoke to those pierced with an anguish, 'whose balsam never grew.' He spoke to the cravings, to the aspirations, to the hopes as well as to the sorrows and the pains of humanity. The generations to come will care little or nothing for our sermons to the times, but they will listen to the sweet, clear voice of the man who preached to the end of Gilead—and Beulah—and the Gates of Day.

May 12, 1910.

CARDINAL VAUGHAN[1]

Mr. Snead-Cox's *Life of Cardinal Vaughan* is, from a literary point of view, the best biography we have read for years. It is admirably proportioned; it is written with remarkable grace and ease; and it is characterised by a candour which never, so far as we see, descends into bitterness. It seems to us that Mr. Snead-Cox undervalues Cardinal Vaughan's literary powers. While allowing that he sometimes wrote noble prose, he says that the Cardinal was often deficient in the sense of words. It is true that his pages do not show the grace and colour, the undulations of fine moods which are evident in Newman, but his style seems to an outsider clear, nervous, and dignified from first to last.

The book is one which ought to be read by Protestants. Cardinal Vaughan did not stand so high in the general opinion as his predecessor, Cardinal Manning. His unfortunate phrase in a letter to Mr. Redmond, 'The triumph of the Government over the Nonconformist opposition,' is admitted to be indiscreet. It stated the fact, however, with great precision. Mr. Snead-Cox

[1] *The Life of Cardinal Vaughan.* By J. G. Snead-Cox. Two volumes. (Herbert and Daniel.)

admits that the Cardinal was thought to be haughty, stern, and aloof in manner. But he deserves study as a born Roman Catholic. Protestants are more interested in the converts to Roman Catholicism, and, if we may judge from the *Tablet* and the *Dublin Review*, so are literary Roman Catholics. But there may be more instruction in the life of a Roman Catholic born and bred, saturated with the doctrines and practices of his faith, and most attracted to those which to us seem most repulsive. Cardinal Vaughan was one such. There is a good deal in him that must be repellent to Protestants, but there is also an element that attracts.

No one is likely in these days to think that we are done with Roman Catholicism. Matthew Arnold was a great believer in the *Zeitgeist*, the Spirit of Time. 'The Spirit of Time,' said he, 'is a personage for whose operations I have the greatest respect. Whatever he does is, in my opinion, of the greatest effect.' Arnold said of Butler's *Analogy*: 'It seemed once to have a spell and a power, but the *Zeitgeist* breathes upon it, and we rub our eyes, and it has the spell and power no longer.' But Arnold's new religion has probably not a single living adherent. The truth is that the *Zeitgeist* is a will-of-the-wisp. When it breathed upon Bunyan he thought that Giant Pagan was dead and that Giant Pope was tottering and crazy. Let the World Missionary Conference say whether Giant Pagan is dead. As for Giant Pope, he embarrasses us at every turn. It might have been thought that the sun would have put out the candles, but we doubt whether Roman Catholicism was ever stronger in such enlightened countries as Germany, Holland, Belgium, and America than it is to-day. We have to recognise the facts, however unwelcome these facts may be.

I

The convert to Popery is attracted by various reasons. There may be those who are captivated by the splendour of those ceremonies in which the mighty intellect of Pascal found only a certain weariness, puerility, and unprofitableness. Certainly Newman and those who went with him were not drawn that way. Lord Acton, who was, after all and in the end of the day, a Roman Catholic, had a passionate admiration for the great Protestant theologian Vinet. This may puzzle at first sight; but, after all, it is not mysterious. For Vinet, in his argument for Christianity, started from the needs of human nature. He questioned his own mind in the face of the Infinite. He found himself drawn right on from consequence to consequence, to the necessity of the Christian revelation. He believed that he had arrived at a point of view from which every detail of Christianity was seen to be in perfect harmony with the clamouring necessities of his own soul. Then, like Thomas at the sight of the Stigmata, he prostrated himself before the Christ and cried, 'My Lord and my God.' At this point men like Newman come in and assert that they need more than the Protestant can give them. The question whether Newman was sceptical is now seen to be largely one of words. Certainly Newman never doubted at any time the truth of the Christian religion, but though he himself might be safe, he believed that the reason of man was so restless, so disposed to devour its own offspring, that it needed more than the guidance of the Holy Scripture and the Holy Spirit. It needed an infallible human authority. Such were the fever, the disorder, the corruption, the restlessness, the insatiableness of human nature, that the spiritual drugs in the possession of the Church at Rome seemed to him a necessity. In particular, there must be an infallible human authority, who could say without possibility of error, This is the revelation of God, and that is not.

Vaughan went through no such process of reasoning. He was born of a good family, and his mother had become a passionate Roman Catholic. She had five daughters and eight sons, and she wanted them all to become priests and nuns. The eldest son was the future Cardinal. For many years she prayed an hour a day that God would call every one of her children to serve Him in the Choir or in the Sanctuary. In the end, all her five daughters entered convents, and of her eight sons six became priests. Even the two who have remained in the world for a time entered ecclesiastical seminaries to try their vocations. It was a principle of Mrs. Vaughan's life never to ask God to send any earthly blessing to those she loved. She said: 'I never ask for any temporal favours for my children.' Herbert Vaughan, to all appearance, never knew a doubt. He had a struggle indeed when he gave up his worldly prospects, which were bright, but that struggle was never with the faith he professed, and, once it was over, he did not look back. A man of this type was necessarily a *persona grata.* Vaughan, to do him justice, seemed quite free from ecclesiastical ambitions. He took up uncoveted tasks like begging for missions from door to door in South America, and founding a missionary college for which he had no money. He also undertook the *Tablet*, a weekly newspaper, and later on the *Dublin Review*, and we gather that these were both troublesome and unremunerative undertakings. But he welcomed with rapture the definition of Infallibility. Every demand for the sacrifice of the intellect was answered with the utmost readiness. When the subject of Papal Infallibility came forward, Vaughan decided in his newspaper to exclude completely any and every expression of the opposite view. 'A search through the correspondence columns of the *Tablet* fails to show a single letter on the side of which in this country Cardinal Newman and the Bishop of Clifton (Dr. Clifford) were the conspicuous exponents.' He considered it an awful responsibility to allow the seeds of doubt to be scattered abroad. Mr. Snead-Cox frankly says the peculiar policy of the *Tablet* at this period made many enemies. 'Its dogmatism, its intolerance of all opposition, its impatience of the attitude of those who dreaded the consequences of a definition, and, above all, its readiness to cry down and discredit its opponents by suggestions of disloyalty, or by open accusations of Gallicanism, alienated the sympathy of a multitude of moderate men.' When certain Anglicans sought for the recognition of their Orders by Rome, Vaughan offered a fierce and scornful opposition. When he received the brief nominating him to be Bishop of Salford, he writes: 'I am grateful for the inspiration to take it at once and lay it upon the Altar before the Tabernacle, and to take it from Our Lord. I then placed it in the hands of the statue of the Immaculate and received it from her, and finally laid it at the feet of St. Joseph and took it thence. I have promised to propagate devotion to the Blessed Sacrament, to our Lady and St. Joseph, and on them I place myself and my whole work of the future.' There are several like passages: 'I do not know what St. Joseph will do for me this month,' he says, towards the end of his life. 'I get something every year from him in March.' He went to see the so-called miracle of the Liquefaction of the Blood of St. Januarius in April. He accepted the 'miracle' completely, declaring that science could not account for it, and that it helped to maintain men's faith in the supernatural, in the power of God, and in the intercession of the saints. It is easy to see that such a man had no relation whatever to the intellectual movement of his time. But he was great in practical affairs. He has left a monument of himself in the new Cathedral at Westminster. He fought hard and, for the time, successfully in the interests of the Roman Catholic schools, spurning the view affirmed in his own paper, that schools paid by the public must be managed by the public. He took more familiar Roman Catholic ground when he said that Roman Catholics would not send their children to any but Roman Catholic schools, and that therefore things must go on. But in America and in many other places this threat has proved of small effect.

II

No one can question that self-renunciation was the rule of Cardinal Vaughan's life. In his early days he was determined to be a missionary, and almost broke his heart when his wish was frustrated. He took for his model the blessed Peter Claver, the seventeenth-century saint, who stayed till death on the burning sands of New Granada, to be the first to welcome the dark slave ship with its freight of human wretchedness, and to bring the message of hope and love to the most miserable and unfriended people in all God's earth. When the days of his strength went, old age still found him at his work, still looking out for the slave ships, still serving the slaves. When death came at last to bring release, Peter Claver was found at his post. The foreign missionaries whom Herbert Vaughan sent out were vowed to consecrate themselves to the service of the heathen, not for a term of years, but without reserve and for ever. 'They go and have gone continuously from Mill Hill for more than thirty years, not into exile, because exile means absence from home, but simply into new homes, to labour there until the end.' Scarcely less rigorous were his rules for the clergy at home. He thought that no priest ought to accumulate money. The idea of a priest leaving property away from his work and the poor he had served was abhorrent to him. The smallest stipend that would keep body and soul together and suffice for efficient work, he held to be ample. Whatever was over from the income of a mission should be spent for the good of the diocese. A full and normal salary for a rector was £50 per annum, and for an assistant priest £40. In no case was the salary payable to an assistant priest to be less than the sum common in many dioceses, £25. He held that the diocesan clergy were a great mendicant order. 'Nothing assuredly is sadder than to see a priest fretting and repining in poverty.' A priest was not to be blamed if he laid by some provision for sickness and old age where there was no common fund for the purpose, but the money must not be bequeathed to friends and relatives. 'It is a scandal to the faithful and a lasting stain on the name of a priest when money given in the service of God, or for the use of His anointed, is hoarded and finally left away from the Church for the enjoyment of a private family.'

What he preached he practised. In the Archbishop's house at Westminster he occupied two small rooms, barely and poorly furnished, and without carpets. In fact, those who knew him best feared that he was suffering from actual privation, and sent him a little money. He kept the money, and it was found in his desk when he died, with a label on which he had written, 'To be returned to Nazareth House after my death.' He insisted on all the privileges of a Cardinal Archbishop, including precedence, and was evidently one of the proudest of men. All he had was given away. He lived and died a lover of evangelical poverty.

It is strange and painful to read that during his last years he wore on his left arm an iron bracelet, with spikes on the inside, which were pressed into the flesh. It was made out of steel wire, and the points were sharp. When it was made to his satisfaction, he told a friend to bring a pair of pliers and to fasten it on the arm so that it could never come off. When that was done, the Cardinal brought his right hand down heavily on the iron circlet and so drove it home. It was cut off his arm after death.

III

We feel more strongly than ever, after reading this book, that the radical error is that of sacerdotalism. We are less able than ever to believe in the dependence of God's people on miracle-working priests. We cannot accept the infallibility of a Church of which the earthly corner-stone may be such an one as Alexander Borgia. Nor can we believe that the true fold of Christ contains none but those who pronounce a solemn anathema on all forms of religion but their own. Dr. Schanz, in his well-known *Christian Apology*, decides that 'what are called *bona-fide* heretics must in all fairness and justice be morally considered members of the one true, visible Catholic Church, though they are not visible in her communion. Thus it remains true that there is no salvation outside of the Church.' But the religion of the New Testament is a religion of unrestricted fellowship with God. The law made nothing perfect; but the bringing in of a better hope did, by the which we draw near to God. We are not come to Mount Sinai, but to Mount Sion and unto the city of the living God, the heavenly Jerusalem, and to an innumerable company of angels, to the general assembly and church of the first-born, and to God the Judge of all, and to the spirits of just men made perfect, and to Jesus the Mediator of the new covenant—and the Forerunner of His people.

June 9, 1910.

PRIMATE ALEXANDER[1]

THE Church of England is by no means poor in great ecclesiastical biographies. Some of them have been criticised as needlessly long and detailed, but on the whole the larger works have justified themselves. For example, the three volumes devoted to Samuel Wilberforce are still invaluable as a contribution to the history of the Church. And the same may be said about the lives of Tait, Magee, and, notwithstanding its extreme dullness, the biography of Dr. Pusey. Nor should we forget to mention Mrs. Creighton's life of her husband.

William Alexander, the eloquent Archbishop of Armagh, was one of the most attractive personalities of his time. Very human, very affectionate, of a glowing temperament and an exuberant eloquence, he was never a man to be overlooked. Hearts went out to him, and his eager tenderness made him very lovable. He was one of the first preachers of his time, one of the very few who can be described as orators of the first rank. He was not a poet in the supreme sense, but he was a very brilliant rhetorician in verse, and at times a little more. It would be idle to say that he was with the

[1] *Primate Alexander, Archbishop of Armagh: A Memoir.* Edited by Eleanor Alexander. (Edward Arnold.)

great poets who sit on peaks above the snow-line. But many of his lines lodge themselves in the heart, and at an advanced age he could write memorial tributes more happily than almost any other poet. By circumstances he was drawn into great battles of the time. First the Irish Disestablishment controversy, then the keen conflicts over the revision of the Prayer-book, and last of all the long contention about Home Rule. Such a man deserved a biography, and we are grateful to Miss Alexander for the readable, interesting, and lovable memoir in which she records the experiences of her father. It would be inhuman to criticise severely a tribute by the truest of daughters, and yet we cannot honestly say that her book is satisfactory. It reminds us of the old Scotswoman who praises the extempore prayers of her minister because they were so 'bonny and throuither and throuither.' Miss Alexander's uniform kindness and charity are disarming, but there is a provoking and amusing want of method about the whole book which was highly characteristic of its subject. We suppose this had to be. We are willing to excuse the sparing references to controversies, although we should have liked to know more about the effects of Disestablishment on the Church of Ireland. The great defect of the book, however, is its slender treatment of Archbishop Alexander's literary work. The very scant list of his books given at the beginning is both deficient and erroneous. We specially deplore the inadequate account of his numerous and valuable contributions to periodical literature. We must also say that the proofs should have been carefully read. The number of mis-spellings and the like is inexcusable. But we gladly pass on to say that the biography is successful, at least, in giving a distinct and personal and attractive impression of its subject.

I

The freshest part of the book is the account of Alexander's early years, and in particular of his time in Oxford.

His father was a parish minister in the Irish Church, and his mother, who was brought up as a Presbyterian, succeeded to a small property which seems to have been burdened. There was a large circle of friends and connections. Miss Alexander has used throughout occasional notes of his life written by her father, and they show the tenacity of his memory and his love. His schooldays were spent at Tonbridge, within a mile of his grand-uncle's place, Somerhill, and the boy seems to have done well. At that time he proposed to be a barrister, and it was said of him that he would have succeeded in any position in life except as a judge. We are tolerably certain that he would never have succeeded as a man of business.

His heart was set on going to Oxford, of which he dreamed waking and sleeping. He entered the

City of Enchantment with awe and rapture, but things very speedily went wrong. He fell in love with a gardener's daughter who cruelly deceived him. There followed months of despair and recklessness, to which he looked back with repentant shame long after. He fell deeply into debt, and his parents cleared him by raising money on already overloaded Irish land. They never murmured, and he made a solemn engagement to repay when he could every penny they had advanced. His mother's unalterable belief in him led to his conversion, and he resolved to dedicate himself to the ministry of the Gospel. With all his weakness at Oxford, he was never insensible to religious impressions, and Newman's influence, then at its height, affected him very deeply. In fact, he determined to join the Church of Rome, and packed up his possessions with the intention of never returning to Oxford. But he came back to Brasenose College, of which he received an honorary fellowship in 1907, when he was eighty-three. Although his time at Oxford was marred by idleness and extravagance, it was not altogether unprofitable. Newman taught him much which he never forgot about literature as well as theology. He must have been in some way a student of great literature. His attainments were not contemptible. He showed himself very early to be that very rare individual, 'a man with a style.' We cannot deny that he is best described as a rhetorician, but there are passages in his essays and sermons of satisfying grandeur and richness and beauty. He possessed something not far short of genius, and an earnest, solemn religiousness marked his best productions.

II

From Oxford he passed at once to parish work in Donegal. He was ordained in 1847, and was a curate till 1850. He began at Derry, where he was born, and from the start he was recognised as a preacher of unusual gifts. Miss Alexander says: 'He had himself been born anew with a deep baptism of fire—mental and bodily suffering; he owed much at this time and throughout life to the noble and restraining influence of his friend and master, Professor Archer Butler. It was with him as guide and counsellor that he was duly ordained priest in Derry Cathedral in 1848.' It might have been mentioned that Butler was then close upon the end of his marvellous career. Probably Alexander himself wrote the short notice of Butler's ordination sermon which appeared in the *Christian Remembrancer*. It was when returning from the ordination that Butler's last death-sickness struck him. Fever rapidly set in, and his mind wandered. One ejaculation was constantly upon his tongue, 'Christ, my Righteousness.' He was in his thirty-fifth year.

The most interesting new fact in the biography is that Archer Butler wooed in vain the lady who became Alexander's wife in 1850. She was indeed a pearl among women. But it is strange that she should have numbered among her lovers the two most brilliant men in the Irish Church. Mrs. Alexander's hymns are the heritage of the universal Church, and of her poem, 'The Burial of Moses,' Tennyson said that he should like to have written it himself. She was singularly attractive, though short-sighted and very shy. William Alexander carried her affections by storm, and, in spite of the usual difficulties, they were married in October 1850. Then began Alexander's true life and ministry, for this was indeed a perfect marriage. They settled in a remote little parish, and after five years they were transferred to Fahan, about nine miles from Derry. It was a romantic home, and very dear to them always. They worked together with great energy and complete harmony in the parish and in the study. It was at Fahan and in Camus Rectory, to which they were promoted, that the Alexanders did their very best literary work. We should have been more than grateful to Miss Alexander if she had helped us to trace that work. But, beyond the barest outline, she tells us nothing. William Alexander followed Archer Butler as the principal contributor to the *Dublin University Magazine*. By examining the old volumes it is possible to see the variety of his gifts and interests, and his singular power of individual writing. Indeed, as a magazine writer he surpassed Archer Butler, though very much below that wonderful man in scholarship and in general power. To the *Christian Remembrancer*, then a valuable quarterly organ of the Church of England, he contributed some of his very best papers. Miss Alexander does not tell us how her father and mother joined in competing for the prize offered at the Crystal Palace for the best poem on Burns, and how they very nearly won it. She says nothing about the noble and magnificent tribute to Archer Butler paid by Alexander in the *Christian Remembrancer*. We long thought that this article must have been written by Dean Church, and there can be no higher compliment. We wish she had said something about Alexander's comments on the Irish revival. Though Alexander was somewhat suspected by his brethren as a High Churchman, he attracted the attention of powerful London critics. Hutton invited him to write in the *Spectator*, and he did so for many years. Froude admired him, and so did Matthew Arnold. Hutton in his generous way took him up in the *Spectator*, and urged his claims to preferment. Norman Macleod enlisted him among the contributors to *Good Words*. He was invited to co-operate in the Speaker's Commentary. We cannot but feel that something should have been said about the characteristics of his expository work. While in point of scholarship and critical power it cannot be compared with that of Westcott and Evans, it is nevertheless very well worth reading. It bears marks of a very wide and varied culture, and many passages are singularly beautiful and poetical. This is specially true of the introduction to the Epistle to the Colossians.

Alexander was invited to preach on special occasions in England, and made a great impression. He might be defined in Archer Butler's words as a preacher 'whose inmost spirit has been busy with the New Testament,' and his splendid gifts were warmly recognised. The result was his appointment in 1867, when he was only forty-three, to the rich Bishopric of Derry.

III

It was as the Bishop of Derry that he became generally known. Alexander and his wife had little time thenceforth for literary work, but their house was a centre of hospitality, and they were soon confronted with the Disestablishment controversy. Of this Miss Alexander says as little as possible, and we shall follow her example. After it life went on with a gentle dignity and peace. The Bishop had a happy time in America, where he lectured and preached. They brought up a family of sons and daughters, and the Bishop paid frequent visits to London. Wherever he preached the church was crowded. Gradually all parties in the Irish Church came to trust him, and when in 1895 his beloved wife passed away streams of love and confidence flowed round him. He was elected Primate of all Ireland by his brother bishops in February 1896, when he had attained the age of seventy-two.

IV

He was to remain Primate till 1911, so that at the time of his resignation he had attained the great age of eighty-six. He retired to Torquay, where he passed away peacefully a few months later.

The Primate's last years were full of love and peace. He mellowed and cultivated the friendship of ministers outside his own Church. While he held fast by the ancient faith, he came to see more clearly than ever that true faith is of the heart, and is compatible with much intellectual defect and confusion. He regretted that he had spoken of Dean Stanley as 'dogma-blind,' and rejoiced in the story of Stanley's deathbed, when he drew himself up on the pillow, stretched out his slender hand, and said to those around him, 'The blessing of God Almighty, the Father, the Son and the Holy Ghost be with you always.' 'Was *that* dogma-blindness ?' said the Primate. From his early years he had exercised himself on the difficulty presented by the divine and exclusive claim of the Church and its apostolic ministry and the existence of Christian holiness outside it. He was not perfectly satisfied with Archer Butler's solution. Archer Butler thought that it was possible to believe 'that every single member of a schismatical congregation has been by God's mercy made a member of Christ, and in the same sacred act registered in heaven a member of the

Church, which is His Body, and yet believe that that congregation is itself as such existing in direct opposition to His will.' This is not easy, and Archer Butler tried another solution by comparing the outside denominations to the little ships that were also with Christ in the tempest, and enjoyed a share in the blessing of calm obtained by the ship that bore Him. The Archbishop ultimately came to the conclusion that Presbyterian orders were valid, and he meant to promote private conferences on the subject. In fact, his last work was a preparation for a discussion on Presbyterian orders. He cultivated tender friendships with Presbyterian ministers, whom he described as 'men of powerful thought and speech.' Before his speech could be delivered he was gathered to the unity of the General Assembly and Church of the First-born.

November 27, 1913.

CHARLES SILVESTER HORNE

THE most sad and unexpected news of Mr. Silvester Horne's sudden death in America has deeply moved the Churches. To his friends, and they were many, it is a bitter personal bereavement with which it is very hard to make terms of peace. His was a spirit indescribably precious. He won from all who knew him both admiration and affection. When he went out to America he was not decided as to his future sphere of work, but he did not doubt that great tasks were before him. He was conscious that his health had been impaired, and not very long ago, in an hour of almost boding reverie, he spoke of the possibilities. Even then, however, it was clear that a certain innermost peace was his, and he soon recovered to talk as brightly and lightly as ever. He was, it seems, in his fiftieth year, but there was a breath of life's morning about him to the very last.

Since he went to the States we have had some communications with him—direct and indirect. After his old manner he threw himself lavishly into labour. He renewed his old friendship with President Woodrow Wilson, whom he knew as Governor of New Jersey. After their first meeting he never doubted Dr. Wilson's great future. 'Some men dominate you by what we are wont to speak of as the magnetism of their personality; and Dr. Wilson simply radiates vitality.' Mr. Horne asked the Governor whether if the Democrats won they would be as friendly toward England as the Republicans had shown themselves. Dr. Wilson replied cordially, and then asked what England was going to do with Ireland. He said that since he had gone into public life he had learned much of the grievances of those Irish who were driven out of Ireland with great cruelty, and whose descendants have not forgotten, nor forgiven, the circumstances of their exile. Mr. Horne replied with a question, 'Suppose we consent to Home Rule?' Dr. Wilson emphatically declared that the passing of Home Rule would sound the death-knell of Irish hostility to Britain so far as America was concerned. When they met again two or three weeks ago the subject was resumed, and the two men were still of the same mind.

Mr. Horne had not arrived at the solution of his perplexities. He saw that it was not possible for him to be at once the minister of a Church and a Member of Parliament. He hesitated between the alternatives. But they did not present themselves so sharply to him as they would to most men. There was never in his mind the faintest thought of ceasing to be a preacher. If his health had been restored and if he had been without pastoral responsibilities he would have preached oftener than ever. He did not draw a line between his religious and his political activities. He included his politics in his religion, and it was in the Name of the Lord Jesus Christ that he spoke the deepest convictions of his soul. We believe that ultimately he would have resumed the pastorate, and that this was the life for which he was best fitted. But his term of earthly service was drawing swiftly to its close, though none of us saw it. He could not measure the limits of his strength or unfailingly keep within them. It was his nature to answer every call, and to encumber himself with labour that was for others rather than for him. So his perplexities were suddenly scattered in the great Morning which rises out of the Eastern Sea.

Alas! that it should be so hard to give a living picture of the dead! How many of us sit down sorrowfully to recall the memories of past intercourse, and all we can find is an attitude, a look, a tone, a word, or it may be a phrase. Such things, at least, are all we can give to others, though our own heart holds what we cannot put into words.

I

Our first impression, and our last, of Silvester Horne is his winsomeness. He resembled Henry Drummond more than any other man we have ever known. His gracious look and manner, his high bearing, his attractive courtesy, and his musical voice impressed and attached every one who met him. He seemed a child of fortune on whom every one smiled.

'None knew thee but to love thee;
None named thee but to praise.'

We believe, and indeed we are sure, that this winsomeness was a natural gift, but he cultivated it carefully. He learned to be patient with the tedious, and to suffer fools gladly. He had a natural and warm interest in every one he met. But there was grace as well as nature in Silvester Horne's charm. Men heard in him the soul's high note, the spiritual voice rising strong and clear over the turmoil. It is not wonderful that he was accepted of his brethren. No Congregational minister was better loved by other ministers than was Mr. Horne. A fact of this kind is always extremely significant, for ministers understand ministers. A proof of his popularity was his early election to the Chair of the Congregational Union. We have heard that when Dr. Dale, of Birmingham, began to fail in health he was recommended to seek a colleague, and his answer was that if he could get Silvester Horne to be his colleague he would gladly agree. Far beyond the Congregational churches—all over the land he won hearts wherever he went, and the tributes already paid to him in America showed that the old enchantment lingered with him to the end.

II

His great and supreme gift, however, was the gift of speech. He was what is called a born speaker, and the man was behind the speech. Preaching was his delight. His Yale lectures dealt, we believe, with the romance of preaching, and told the story of great Gospel victories in the past. His own beliefs were deeply evangelical. He was broad and sympathetic; he welcomed thought and study; he was never tied to forms. But his faith was an anchor cast into the deep sea, and it held fast. Those who imagined that Mr. Horne habitually preached on the political controversies of the day did not know the man. In the pulpit he dealt chiefly with the high and solemn mysteries of faith. He never made any special study of style. He did not trouble about the right verbal garment for his thought, but he was a master of lucid exposition. He was very careful in his preparation, and he spoke right on. When Dr. Dale introduced him to the church at Kensington in 1889 he pleaded with the congregation to allow their young minister a place in their prayers. 'Pray for him that his courage may be high; that his faith may have the fortitude of granite rocks; that the fires of his love for God may burn higher and higher, and with a clearer flame as the months and years pass by; that his zeal for your righteousness and your full realisation of the Christian redemption may grow in intensity; that his joy in the vision of God may become fuller and fuller.' Shall we not say that these prayers were offered and answered?

What William James said of Emerson is true of Silvester Horne: 'The hottest side of him is his Nonconformist persuasion, and if his temper could ever verge on common irascibility it would be by reason of the passionate character of his feelings on this point.' He had a burning interest in the social problem, and his political beliefs were those of an advanced Radical. But what strikes us most as we think of him is the intensely religious character of his total thought.

We have all been accustomed to say that he excelled chiefly as a platform speaker. At his best he was the equal of any man in this country when dealing with the problems of life and action. He could rise on occasion to almost matchless eloquence. Victory beamed from his brow. He believed in God and man and woman. Through the worst squalor he saw the transfiguration. Though capable of a very lonely courage, he was by nature sane. He hated revolution, and it was this that made him so urgent in his pleading for reform. History had taught him that evils should be checked in time before they became past remedy save by violence. What was peculiar in Silvester Horne was that he could not draw any distinction between his politics and his religion. He believed that nothing could save the State except that Christianity which is its only bulwark. He had an intense belief in conversion. He longed to make his church a place in the atmosphere of which no sceptic could come and remain a sceptic. There were mysteries into which his vision did not pierce, but what he saw he saw clearly.

III

It is worth while to dwell on this, for it was this faith that was the key to Silvester Horne's life. He was blamed for making a political meeting one of his services on Sunday. He was also blamed for entering the House of Commons as a Christian minister. He was almost ludicrously unable to see the meaning of these charges. To him every political question was at its roots a religious question. When he went into the House of Commons what impressed him was the amount of time devoted to arguing religious questions. He thought that there was no place where a really Christian minister would be more likely to feel at home. There was the subject of slavery in the Congo or the Putumayo. There were the relations of Church and State in respect of marriage. There was a great Home Rule issue, renewing the old No-Popery agitation. There was Welsh Disestablishment, involving the positive argument for a free church in a free State. Temperance Bills were asked for by religious men on religious grounds. The Churches were not silent on the white slave traffic, and they ought not to be silent on the reconstruction of the Poor Law. The rights of trade unionists, the duty of insuring workers against ill-health and unemployment were to him profoundly religious questions.

He went so far as to lay down a programme for the Churches. There were certain measures in regard to which the Church had to let her mind be known or abdicate all claim to moral leadership.

Among these were Licensing Reform, the Reconstruction of the Poor Law, a Living Wage, Divorce, the Arrest of Gambling, and, above all, International Peace. He suggested that 'the Churches should agree to carve out, as it were, of the general body of political questions certain problems as to whose social and moral character there can be no dispute, and frankly claim and freely exercise the right and the duty to deal with these questions in the light of Christian ethics.'

In private, and we believe also in public, he vindicated a theory of Church and State which we have often told him amounted to Hildebrandism. He really believed that the Church should rule the State, that the children of light should govern the children of the world. Hildebrand was a Pope who convinced himself that the Church was entitled in its own nature to ascendancy over the State, and carried the conviction into action. He quarrelled with Henry IV., and summoned him to appear at Rome and be judged. The Emperor convened a Synod of the German Church at Worms, which declared the Pope to have forfeited his high place and called on him to come down. The undaunted Pope excommunicated the great uncrowned Emperor, interdicted him from ruling his kingdoms of Italy and Germany, and absolved all his Christian subjects from their oaths. Let Dr. Taylor Innes tell the story: 'The spiritual stroke paralysed the unwieldy secular power. The great northern bishops shrank from the side of their excommunicated lord; Swabia and Carinthia prepared to follow the Saxon revolt against him, and most of his princes called upon Henry to submit. Suddenly, in the midst of the fierce winter of 1077, the monarch crossed the Alps to seek absolution, and made his way to where Gregory dwelt as guest of the Countess Matilda in her fortress of Canossa. For three days successively the lord of the world stood from morning to evening in the outer court of the castle, in woollen shirt and with feet bare, petitioning in vain for admittance. Not till the fourth day was absolution granted to his weeping submission. The Pope lost not a moment in publishing the astounding transaction to the world.'

But Hildebrand went too far and died rejected. His last words were: 'I have loved righteousness and hated iniquity; and therefore I die in exile.'

We have dwelt on this subject to show the originality and daring of Mr. Horne's thought. In essence he may have been right. The future may yet vindicate him. One art he never learned—he did not know how to husband the taper. Alas! there are many like him, and their light goes out too soon and leaves us in a dark sorrow. The taper may be husbanded meanly and selfishly. It may also be husbanded with humble faith and pious care. We did not know how dear Silvester Horne was to us till we lost him. But we have not lost him, for he lived his short earthly life in the power of the life of the Eternal Son.

May 7, 1914.

THE POWER OF KNOWLEDGE: PROFESSOR FLINT[1]

THE biography of Dr. Flint follows hard upon that of Dr. Fairbairn. Both books enforce with overwhelming effect the truth that Knowledge is Power. It was their extraordinary learning that singled out Flint and Fairbairn from their contemporaries. Both had manifold gifts, of speech, of intellectual energy, or religious devotion. But it was their supremacy in knowledge that impressed men's minds. They spent long and lonely hours of study in comparative obscurity, but once they had accomplished their tasks and displayed their resources the most jealously locked doors fell suddenly open.

When Tennyson died in 1892 a very able critic of the time said: 'It is a mark of our age that we are replacing all the old fissures between classes by the bridgeless chasm between the cultivated and the ignorant; that while we talk of the quality there has grown up a secret sign, the modulation of the voice, by which, in the darkest night or in the thickest cloud, the educated can and do recognise one another.' This statement would now need to be much modified. It is true that the unlearned, the half learned, and the learned do homage to the very few who are really masters.

[1] *The Life of Robert Flint, D.D., LL.D.*, by Donald Macmillan, M.A., D.D. (Hodder and Stoughton.)

I

Dr. Macmillan, whose skill as a biographer is already well proved, has written a book of which it can be unreservedly said that it is worthy of its subject. Higher praise we cannot imagine. We admire the skill with which the facts are arranged, the just proportion of the chapters, the wisdom of the comments, and, above all, the becoming spirit of affectionate reverence which pervades the book. Dr. Macmillan does not tire us with the dreary drip of incessant panegyric, but he knows, and makes it clear that he knows, how great and noble was the man he is dealing with, how worthy, influential, and Christian was the career which it is his lot to describe. If any fault is to be found, it is a fault on the side of virtue. Dr. Macmillan has modestly assigned certain chapters of his biography to Dr. Wenley and Dr. James Lindsay—Dr. Wenley dealing with Flint as a philosopher, and Dr. Lindsay discussing his works on Theism. Dr. Wenley is always racy and suggestive, while Dr. Lindsay has shown himself an accomplished student of the Theistic controversy. We cannot help saying, however, that we wish Dr. Macmillan had written these chapters himself. He is well qualified to do so, and the result would have been more satisfactory. For Dr. Wenley often wanders from his subject, and Dr. Lindsay was not called upon to characterise works on Theism subsequent to Flint—not even his own. There is also an assumption of finality in

Dr. Lindsay's judgments which provokes rebellion. Still, the chapters make good reading and are written in a becoming spirit. For the rest we can only repeat our praise in the hope that many students will read this memoir with profit and delight. No recent book of the kind has pleased us half so well.

We do not propose to summarise Dr. Macmillan's volume, but rather to supplement what he has given us with a few notes on Flint's personality and works. In doing so we may at least claim as title an almost lifelong and reverential appreciation of this great man, philosopher, and divine.

II

Dr. Flint's father was a shepherd in Dumfriesshire, but soon became a business man in Glasgow. He was evidently remarkable for his piety and his intellectual vigour. He was a devoted member of the Free Church, and it might have been expected that his son would follow him. It seems, however, that Flint was alienated from the Free Church after the age of twenty by some miserable heresy squabble involving Glasgow divinity students. He thus turned to the Church of Scotland. Flint's powers were more quickly discovered than Fairbairn's. He was a distinguished student, and he devoted himself with much earnestness to mission work in the slums of Glasgow. There he came into contact with the radiant spirit of Norman Macleod, an experience for which he never ceased to thank God. Flint had developed early striking powers of speech, and he was settled as minister of the East Church in Aberdeen in 1859, when he was only twenty-five. It is touching to read that he took his parents with him, and that they remained with him to the end. His father remained a Free Churchman, and it sounds almost incredible to be told that during the time of his residence in Aberdeen he never worshipped in his son's church. So far was this from offending Flint that his father was head of the household, and continued to conduct family worship even in the time when the son had become Professor of Divinity in Edinburgh University. Dr. Macmillan says well: 'The father remained the head of the house until he died. There is surely something touching and beautiful in all this. One of the greatest scholars of his day, a man of world-wide reputation, the leading theologian of Scotland, sits humbly at the family table and kneels reverently at prayer while his aged father, a simple peasant, conducts the devotions of the household.'

Flint was very successful in Aberdeen, and also in a Fifeshire parish, Kilconquhar, where he remained for a few years. But it was obvious that he would find his place in a Professor's Chair. Accordingly he became, in 1864, at the age of thirty, Professor of Moral Philosophy in the University of St. Andrews. The Chair had been occupied by men like Chalmers and Ferrier, and it lost none of its dignity when held by Flint. Indeed the impression he made is proved by the saying of A. K. H. B.: 'There can hardly ever have been a better Professor in any University in this world. A quiet, recluse student, by pure force of high qualities he gained extraordinary popularity with the undergraduates.'

During his time in St. Andrews Flint studied without ceasing. Gradually and silently he acquired all the languages necessary for his purpose, and read as few men have ever read. But he did not become known to the world of letters until 1874, when he published his book on *The Philosophy of History*.

III

The appearance of this book was an event. It is not too much to say that it astonished the world of letters. John Morley devoted an article to the volume in the *Fortnightly Review*, of which he was then the editor. He gave the highest praise to Flint's 'gift of being candid and fair in the highest degree.' He spoke of his 'thorough justice of intellect.' He also laid stress on the learning of the treatise. 'His reading has been most extensive, and the list of his authors, so far as France and Germany is concerned, is remarkably complete.' George Eliot praised the book 'for its thorough fairness from his point of view and masterly grasp of the subject.' Equally gratifying was the recognition from scholars and thinkers on the Continent. Germans, Frenchmen, Italians, Spaniards, all reviewed the book with the highest praise, and the position of the author as one of the first scholars of his time was thenceforth assured.

Dr. Macmillan says that the very able article on the book which appeared in the *Spectator* 'is believed to have been written by Sir Frederick Pollock, at the time a young barrister in London.' He ought to know, but we have always believed, and still believe, that the article was written by James Macdonell of the *Times*. We know, at any rate, that Macdonell, who wrote a very elaborate article on the same subject in the *North British Review*, was most keenly interested in the treatise. In fact, his whole mind was occupied by it for the time. Both Flint and Macdonell were very intimate friends of a gifted Baptist minister in Aberdeen, the Rev. G. S. Mee, and if we are not mistaken they were personally acquainted. Macdonell was profoundly impressed by the provincialism of Scottish theology. No voice from a Scottish Chair reached the ear of Europe. When Flint appeared 'in shining armour dressed' it was recognised at once that this was a philosopher and divine first among the foremost. Macdonell hardly did justice to Flint's learning—that is, he thought that Flint had paid attention to men who did not deserve it. He considered that Flint was most effective when he was most controversial. Differing from Morley, he considered that Flint's criticism of Comte was conspicuously able and powerful. Morley understood better than Macdonell the vital importance of exhaustive knowledge. Flint's outstanding merit was that he never allowed his knowledge to deaden the ceaseless activity of his intellect. Flint was appointed Professor of Theology in the University of Edinburgh, and from that time ranked with A. B. Davidson as one of the two really commanding influences in the Divinity Halls of Scotland.

IV

Passing over Flint's precious contributions to Apologetics, the influence of which it would be impossible to overrate, we pass on to say a word on his theology. He held firmly to Catholic Christianity. There was in his time a strong Broad Church party in the Church of Scotland. Its leaders were able and eloquent men, but they were not learned, and Flint would scarcely be numbered in their camp. His attitude reminds us of Westcott's remark on *Essays and Reviews*—that they were to be refuted by a deeper learning. Flint was the last man to bring charges of heresy in a reckless way. As a rule he understated his case, and was perfectly calm and courteous even while he planted his most telling blows. His temper, naturally sweet and equable, burst into fierce flames of wrath wherever he saw injustice. But in the main he was patient, candid, and forbearing to a degree. The narrow Evangelicals could not claim him, but he was to the last Evangelical. He held that a deep creed lay at the very core of Christianity. Christianity is something more than the emotions of wonder, love and awe. These are followed by reflection, and the reflection must build up a creed. In Flint's view it is revelation, and revelation only, that gives us the means of steering on unknown seas. With the help of revelation the human mind is able to analyse its trust in Christ, to meditate on the apparent incompatibility of Divine and human knowledge; on the humility and supremacy of our Lord; on His omnipotence and His death on the Cross. Flint's sermons, of which many have been published, had an intense effect when delivered, though they are very quietly written. They are for the most part timeless. There are preachers who owe their freshness and their impact on the mind of hearers to the fact that they deal with themes which at the time are uppermost in the hearts of men. Flint's sermons were expressions of the deeper mind and feeling of the speaker and charged with the memory and reality of living emotion.

V

We take leave to make a note on Dr. Flint's treatise on Socialism, which was published in 1894. Though the situation has much altered, the book still deserves to be read. Flint never lost his early interest in the condition of the people. He wrote on the subject with the heat of a living and beating heart. Souls that are chiefly fed on books are apt to grow up, like plants in the dark, weak and colourless, without the direct stimulus of the sun of life.

But Flint cared for life as well as for books, else he had never interpreted books so well. In reading it one is more impressed than ever with the tremendous learning at the back of every sentence, and the wealth of knowledge of which one feels that he has only seen a glimpse. In this respect Flint was without a rival among students of the subject. His position is that of a generous individualism. He believes that Socialism in every form spells slavery. The evils of society are to be mitigated by charity and by cautious legislative reform. As Dr. Macmillan does not quote it, we may give Flint's views on Old Age Pensions. The following sentence seems to anticipate Mr. Lloyd George's scheme :—

> 'When men have worked steadily and faithfully during the years of their strength in any useful occupation, a system securing for them pensions in old age would only, I think, be the realisation of a genuine right which they had fairly and honourably earned. Those who bring about the realisation of this right will deserve to rank high among the benefactors of the working classes and among true patriots.'

VI

Here we must pause. Mrs. Burnett Smith contributes to Dr. Macmillan's memoir a delightful account of Flint's happy life with his devoted and accomplished sister. She allows us to add that their acquaintance began when she consulted him about one of her books, *Maitland of Laurieston.* In this she endeavoured to bring her hero back from the path of agnosticism into the path in which he was reared. Flint gave her his advice and among other things he wrote, ' Remember that religion or faith can only be lost or won through the affections.' Flint had no arrogance in his manner; he was the friendliest and simplest of men; but there was a certain dignity about him which only the most obtuse could miss. One had a feeling of awe in the presence of such learning and power. From his lips the most commonplace opinion was weighty. One knew that the judgment had been passed through the fire. Dr. Flint retired from the Chair, which he so long adorned, in 1903, and was able to publish two books more ere the end came. If at the last his luminous intellect was partially dimmed, and his eloquent voice no longer moved multitudes, he was at peace. He bore all he had to bear with fortitude and dignity, and the most loving care surrounded him to the very last.

December 17, 1914.

FATHER STANTON: THE CENTRE OF COMMUNION[1]

We give a most cordial welcome to the handsome volume which contains an abiding memorial to one of the least ostentatious and most powerful of London ministries. For close on fifty years, without receiving a penny in the way of earthly reward, Father Stanton preached to great and deeply impressed crowds at St. Alban's, Holborn. He was a very High Churchman and, as was right and proper, his special views are well represented in this book. But he attracted multitudes who in various respects were more or less at issue with him. They found themselves none the less in true accord with the Gospel which he proclaimed. He himself was also indebted to preachers who were not of his own school. As Father Russell tells us, he had a great admiration for Phillips Brooks, but he found more help in Spurgeon, whom he loved, and—towards the end—in Dr. Parker, whose powers as an expositor he placed very high.

I

We can understand why Father Stanton's friends should feel sensitive about the effect which dis-

[1] *Father Stanton's Last Sermons in St. Alban's, Holborn.* Edited, with a preface, by E. F. Russell, M.A., St. Alban's, Holborn. (Hodder and Stoughton.)

courses like those contained in this volume may have upon the public. Father Russell himself says: 'To some of us it seemed as if the influence of the spoken words was so inseparably, so inextricably bound in with the energy and the charm of the speaker's remarkable presence and personality—face, voice, grace of manner—that to divide his words from him would be like the dividing of body and soul: it would leave the separated words motionless, pale, and dead.' Also, the sermons are shorthand reports, uncorrected by the speaker. But we are sure that these misgivings will be completely dispelled when the sermons are read. Behind the easy and spontaneous fluency of Father Stanton's eloquence there was the most anxious labour, care, and preparation. Father Stanton prepared every sermon as thoughtfully and precisely as if he held his long experience of no account, and he has left six quarto volumes containing elaborate outlines of over a thousand sermons. It is true, indeed, that for those who were accustomed to hear him nothing can compensate for that piercing glance, for the sight of the pilgrim soul in that changing face, for that varied rise and flow of utterance which characterised the preacher. And yet we are sure that the winsomeness of this book, its charm, its fullness, and its divine simplicity, which is the first step of nature and the last of art, will command the gratitude and the joy which come from hearing a true voice.

Father Stanton's eloquence was the eloquence that comes from a living fountain of love. His sermons are full of fine thought and pure theology. But their main characteristic is their evangelicalism. The essence and core of his faith were an intense and personal love for Christ. He was possessed by a most earnest and, on the whole, a deep and catholic faith, and the points in which we differ from him are small in proportion to those which command our heartiest sympathy. For the true meeting place of divided Christians is not, as many think vainly, in the circumference of the creed, but in its burning centre. No man of his time preached more earnestly, or with a more simple heart, the doctrines of conversion and of communion with the living Redeemer. He never travelled far from Calvary, and he understood well that Calvary, as he says, goes back into the very Being of God. 'Calvary has no date; it lies right back in the truth of God. The redemption of mankind is as old as God Himself, so do not you ever say that our faith is not old. Our religion is like God, from everlasting to everlasting. There never was a time when redemption was not in the Mind of God, and there never is or will be a time when redemption will not be in the Mind of God. We put Calvary so many years back, but we are thinking of Calvary under the ticking of the clock. Put yourself into eternity, and Calvary has no beginning and no end, either in time or application.' So he continued to say, 'Behold the Lamb of God, the Lamb slain from the foundation of the world, and slain to its final judgment.'

It is with a great refreshment of spirit that we come across some of Spurgeon's favourite quotations. As for the coming to Christ there is but one way. There is to be no manner of delay. 'Do you feel your need of Christ? If you feel your need, you will be in earnest.'

> 'Let not conscience make you linger,
> Nor of fitness fondly dream;
> All the fitness He requireth
> Is to feel your need of Him.
> This He gives you,
> 'Tis the spirit's rising beam.'

We come to Christ as the leper came, bowed by his reproach. There is no preparation. There is no hanging back. There is the approach and the welcome and the covenant and the blessed and eternal peace. These fifty sermons range over the Christian year, but Christ, and Calvary, and Resurrection, and the Descent of the Holy Ghost make up nearly all the themes. We like very much the meditation on the Seven Words. The preacher ventures to cherish a hope even for the thief who received no promise, the thief who blasphemed and was silent. Even that great outcast of Israel may have been gathered in. 'Silence reigns over him. He passes away in silence. The Holy Scripture gives us not a word about his end. Do you know nothing about him? No—nothing about him. . . . I have no warrant to tell you he was saved, but I have no warrant to tell you he was damned.'

And, however this may be, it is always true that there is life in a look from the Crucified. When the suffering thief turned round and looked on Christ and saw Christ looking at him, and asked his Saviour to give him remembrance, the Lord Who reigned from the Tree gave him something more than a remembrance. He gave him Paradise.

Readers of William Law will understand us when we say that Father Stanton preached not Christian redemption, but *the* Christian redemption. This is the line between false and true Evangelicalism.

II

It is this strong grasp of Christ, living and dying, rising and reigning, that brings together in strange ways the children of God's divided Israel. Of this we venture to give one or two illustrations from biography.

The great Evangelical movement in Scotland, which had visible manifestation in the Disruption, had singular points of contact with the Tractarian Movement in England, although the leaders on each side were ignorant of each other and failed to acknowledge it. One of the very ablest men in the Scottish Free Church was Dr. James Walker, of Carnwath. Dr. Walker left little save a really brilliant fragment on Scottish Church history, and he was for many years an invalid incapable of work. In more favourable circumstances he might have been a leader of theological thought. As a student he was a Tory and a Moderate, but he changed, and became a passionately convinced Evangelical. This change seems to have manifested itself decidedly after a visit to England in the early 'forties. He was deeply interested in and attracted by the Oxford Movement. The effect of this Movement upon him was to make him immensely more serious and earnest, so that his whole family became affected by his spirit. His interest in Tractarianism led him to the study of the Fathers, and with many of their writings he became specially familiar. The influence lasted with him, for he admired the saints of the Early Church and Middle Ages and passed through an ascetic experience. He had early manifested his taste for Church history; he was at home in every department of it—early, mediæval, Reformed, Puritan, Covenanting. His biographer says that in later years these various types, so diverse, were blended in him in strange harmony. In after life he was a Presbyterian High Churchman.

We may refer also to the experience of Coventry Patmore. There is something about Patmore that is very repellent though not easily defined. But he understood what Christianity was. In early days, he tells us, it came to him to consider 'how it would be if Christianity were true, and if there were not only a loving and governing God but one Who was also Man, and so capable of according to me the most intimate communion with Himself.'

Young Patmore went to Edinburgh to visit some friends when the Free Church was new-born. These friends were very pious members, and were the first religious persons he had ever had anything to do with. He says: 'I was at first greatly delighted with this atmosphere, and the warmth with which I communicated my own aspirations much interested my new friends in me; but the inequality of my moods startled and somewhat shocked one of my aunts, who told me that my strange alternations of ardent effort and despondent indifference reminded her of Saul.' Later on he says, referring to the intense Protestant feeling of the Free Church: 'The only sincere and effective religion I had come across in the world had been that of persons to whom the name of the Catholic religion was an abomination. My aunts had the sincerity, sweetness, and devotion of Catholic saints—and such I hope they were—and while in Edinburgh I had come into personal contact with some of the chief of the ministers of the Free Kirk, which was just then in its first fervour. The devotion of these men was unmistakable; and my consciousness had no concrete evidence to counterpoise what I supposed to be the testimony of such characters.' Patmore, as is well known, became a Roman Catholic, a sincere though somewhat perverse member of the communion.

We could add to these instances, but we content ourselves with one more. In his beautiful little biography of R. A. Suckling, the saintly Isaac Williams tells us that some of the sermons by Mr. Suckling which he published in the first edition were in a measure derived from printed matter. Two in particular were from a late minister of the Free Kirk in Scotland. There was no plagiarism in the business. Mr. Suckling selected the sermons as expressive of his own mind, adapted them, and interspersed them with passages unmistakably his own. Still, the communion of spirit is remarkable. If we are not very much mistaken, the sermons were by McCheyne, but at this moment we are unable to make sure.

III

We feel that we have failed to do anything like full justice to this powerful and winning volume. We could have desired to say more of its childlike faith and something of its deep pathos, accompanied by touches of that humour which is never very far away when pathos is present. Readers will feel, as hearers did, that they are neither argued nor thundered into conviction. The preacher speaks with authority from a valid experience, and he enters very fully into the cares, the perplexities, and the sorrows of his listeners. His book is not encumbered with impossible or obsolete orthodoxies. But experience has shown, and will continue to show, that when certain truths and facts are abandoned, the sovereign and supreme love for Christ, which is the bond of believers, cannot be maintained. The human mind in individual cases may harbour for long contradictory beliefs. But logic has its way at length, and outside of those to whom Christ has ceased to be Very God of Very God, this ardour is chilled and killed. It is the business of us all to labour for that outward and visible unity of the Church which is clearly taught in the New Testament, but we will reach it, not by the adoption of formulas which may have a hundred meanings, but by the patient search into those beliefs which are necessary if Christ is to be held up as the Lover, the Redeemer, the Prophet, the Priest, and the King of souls.

January 13, 1916.

THE CENTENARY OF FREDERICK ROBERTSON

Frederick Robertson, of Brighton, that good soldier of Jesus Christ, that just and faithful knight of God, that royal preacher, was born on February 3, 1816—exactly a hundred years ago.

'And now, I pray you, do your part of the work quickly,' said Dr. Hamilton of Leeds, as he put the last sheets of his *Life of John Ely* into the hands of the publisher, 'for ministers are soon forgotten.' This is only too true, but Robertson is not forgotten. His Brighton ministry lasted but a few years, and it was exercised in a shabby little chapel holding some five hundred people. He published in his brief lifetime only one sermon, and that, strange to say, was on the death of Queen Adelaide. Since he died, however, multitudes have been moved by him as by no other teacher, and there is that in Robertson's sermons which may keep them alive for another hundred years. Brighton has not been without her share of gifted preachers. We recall James Vaughan, Wade Robinson, Alfred Norris, and others. But the chief glory of the Brighton pulpit is, and will remain, the minister whose centenary we are recalling.

I

It is not at all our purpose to attempt an estimate of Robertson either as a man or as a preacher or as a theologian. This has been done a thousand times, and often very effectively. We wish rather to add something to the very little that is known about him outside the Life by Stopford Brooke. His own family, though the materials were abundant, decided at last that they would not use them for a supplementary volume. Considering his amazing genius and personal charm, he had very few intimate friends, and not one of these was a man of high distinction. He was a solitary spirit, and no writer of his rank has ever dwelt more poignantly on the misery of loneliness. He belonged to no party in the Church. Though he had a bare acquaintance with Kingsley and Maurice, he was not in any sense a member of their school. He came to repudiate the Evangelical party, in which he had been nurtured, with a strange bitterness, and with the High Church party he had little or no sympathy. One sometimes imagines that it was his great misfortune not to meet and cope with minds on the same footing as his own. He hammered out his own theology, and yet it was not so original as he imagined it to be. In these days he would certainly be described as a Liberal Evangelical. But Liberal Evangelicals were then very few, and his mind would not have stood still. He would have gone further in directions which no one has a right to indicate.

Robertson, however, did come to some extent into contact with the larger world. He was one of those whom the unhappy Lady Byron drew into the circle of her kindness, and there was at one time a probability that her biography and papers would be edited by Robertson. Lady Byron had many protégés. Sometimes her friendship with them was steadfast, sometimes even it grew. With George Macdonald, for instance, she remained in the strongest spiritual communion, and, as one of the dedications of his books shows, he loved her with a love stronger than death. He has drawn her character, as she appeared to him, in Lady Bernard, in his novel, *The Vicar's Daughter*.

R. H. Hutton was for a short time one of her acquaintances. She helped in providing funds for the publication of his *National Review*. The connection was short-lived, and Hutton wrote of her sudden changes from cordial to icy moods, and her unfortunate errors of judgment. These he thought extenuated by the terrible sufferings she went through. We shall probably never know what Lady Byron really was, for we believe her representatives will not allow her writings to be published. Through her Hutton came to hear Robertson preach, at the time when he was struggling out of the Unitarian into the Trinitarian faith. Happily he has left some notes of the impressions made upon him by Robertson, and as such notes are very few, we are sure our readers will thank us for them.

Hutton knew Theodore Parker, and he used to

contrast the brightness of Parker with the sadness of Robertson. He attributed the difference to the fact that Parker, who died of consumption, had all the sanguineness which often marks that disease, while Robertson very early gave signs of that painful malady of the brain to which he succumbed. For Robertson as a man and as a preacher he had the warmest admiration. On first hearing him he was specially impressed by a certain effect of chivalry and romance which was inseparable from Robertson, and which, while it greatly increased his fascination over the minds of others, filled himself with distrust and even sometimes with alarm. Robertson thought that he was merely stirring a superficial sentiment into activity when his desire was to reach the conscience and the will. He was doubtless mistaken. This was not the final effect of his influence, but it was the first point on which his influence fastened itself in the minds of his hearers.

'This half-ideal and romantic aspect of his influence was due to a number of causes; a little perhaps to the symmetry of his figure and his faultless features; more to the half-commanding air and military carriage expressing, if not resulting from, his strong passion for a soldier's life, and his eager preparation for it in youth; still more to the hectic expression of nervous suffering which his constitutional delicacy, his liability to strong excitement, and the lassitude which followed it, left almost always more or less traced upon his face; and very much also to that delicate poetic sensibility to physical influences which always speaks out plainly in the face, and that, too, in a way to invite even more sympathy than the lines of those deeper and more permanent cares which never vary with the expression of the moment. All these causes together produced a temperament and an expression which it was singularly difficult to connect with the commonplace framework of daily life. A high-strung tension of nerve, due certainly in some measure to disease, seemed to mark his face even in repose. The slight undercurrent of fever which was, with him, due to physical delicacy, heightened the moral colours of his mind, and gave them that air of ideality and romance for which the young are always thirsting. Not only his extraordinary eloquence, but all the constituents which went to make that eloquence, conspired to deepen this impression.'

We count ourselves happy in being able to reproduce this description, which somehow seems to bring Robertson nearer to us than any other we have read.

II

His devoted son, the late Mr. Charles Robertson, of the Foreign Office, said to us more than once that the omission he most regretted in Brooke's biography of his father—of which he highly approved in the main—was that it did not bring out the fact that he was essentially a Scotsman. His father was one of the Robertsons of Struan, and his mother was one of the old Scottish family of the Bethunes. His father, being a Captain in the Royal Artillery, had to move from place to place, and so it happened that Robertson was born in London. But he was, in everything but the name, a Scottish Celt, and the fact is significant and illuminating in no ordinary degree. Much of the continual controversy which unhappily occupied him was due to the fact that his lifelong passion was, not to be a minister, but to be a soldier. There is something very painful in the continual thwartings of his desire. It is likely enough that in the Army during peace time he would have been unhappy. But when he was persuaded to study for the ministry, he knew, and he never ceased to feel, that he had sacrificed the dearest wish of his heart. The sacrifice proved to be altogether gratuitous. Within three weeks of his matriculation a letter arrived from the Horse Guards offering him a cornetcy in the 3rd Life Dragoons—the same regiment which in the wars of the Punjab a few years later greatly distinguished itself. But he had put his hand to the plough and would not withdraw it. At the same time, he could never be brought to affirm that he was satisfied with what he had done. 'Wait,' was always his answer; 'some day I will tell you.' The soldierly feeling entered everywhere into his preaching. He was always teaching discipline, the braving of danger, the duty of unhesitating military obedience towards a leader, the stern truth of retribution. He foresaw the Armageddon in which we are now living—foresaw it without fear. Very early during his residence in Germany he marked the hatred of the Germans for the British people. He had an immense faith in the courage of his countrymen. Some of his most eloquent writing relates to this. His rapturous joy in a military career breaks out when he is describing, for example, the glorious death of the heroes of Trukee. He wished to die sword in hand against the invaders :—

'If a foreign foot be planted on our sacred soil . . . terrible as the first reverses might be, when discipline could be met only by raw enthusiasm—thanks to gentlemen who have taught us the sublime mysteries of capital in lieu of the old English superstitions of Honour and Religion, they may yet chance to learn that British chivalry did not breathe her last at Moodkee, or Ferozeshah, or Sobraon, or Goojerat, or Meeanee, or Hyderabad.'

He gloried in the news of the *Birkenhead* :—

'God forbid that we should glory in our country's wealth, her renown, or her military successes, merely as such; God forbid that we should glory in aught of hers, save in that English spirit of Duty and of Sacrifice on which are stamped so unmistakably the lineaments of the Redeemer's Cross. It was this which constituted the real force of that sublime battle-cry which preceded one of the most terrific lessons ever given to the world by the lips of her artillery, and told men wherein lay the might and the majesty of a country which expects of her chosen sons, in the hour of death and danger, not that every man shall save his own life—nor that every man shall seek his own glory—but that "every man shall do his own duty." . . . I do love and honour my dear old country with all my heart and soul; her sons cannot sing, paint, nor carve, but they can die at their posts silently, without thinking that "forty centuries are looking down upon them" from the Pyramids.'

'I felt,' he said, discussing Macbeth, and Macduff's revenge, 'I felt as if to have a firm grip of a sword in a villain's heart were the intensest rapture this earth has to give—the only thing that such as Macduff had worth living for.'

This temper of antagonism, heightened no doubt by approaching disease, made him fiercely impatient of criticism and opposition. We have no intention whatever of taking up dead controversies. We doubt whether Robertson made any very original or remarkable contribution to theology, but his wrath against the Evangelicals, to whom he had once belonged, seems unreasonable in view of the fact that he undertook practically to correct all the schools, and teach them that their way of holding religion was false and base. He suffered, but to the last he was a formidable antagonist, and at this distance we can see that on his side, and on the side of his opponents, there is much to regret, much to forgive, and something to excuse. They were nearer one another than they knew.

III

We would say, in a word, that Robertson's work was done in the most glorious of all spheres of work —the preaching of the Gospel of Christ. It was he as much as any other who reminded the world, and has kept reminding it, that there may be as much originality and genius in sermons as in anything else. The lesson is unspeakably precious. For the rest, we recall the sad, heroic story of his death. He suffered from what he seemed to feel most— bitter and unremitting physical pain. He was partially paralysed, pitifully emaciated. Worse than that was the prostration of all mental force, the obliteration of large spaces from the memory, and the loss of all power of attention. The disease was in his brain, and it killed him. His mother, his wife, and one friend, with his physician, watched over him, seeking by every means in their power to alleviate his sufferings; but he could not bear to be touched. 'I cannot bear it,' he said; 'let me rest. I must die. Let God do His work.' These were his last words. He died when he was little over thirty-eight years. A nobler Christian gentleman never appeared among us.

February 3, 1916.

DR. ALEXANDER WHYTE

DR. ALEXANDER WHYTE died in his sleep, at Hampstead, on Thursday. He had completed his eighty-fourth year. In the few months of his residence at Hampstead he had to bear suffering, but he had many consolations and supports. As the days went on he became more and more mellow and radiant. The occasional rapture of his face still bore witness that his thought was far away in the heavenly places with Christ. Those who were near him knew the meaning of every light that passed or lingered in his countenance. He was often marked with memorial suffering, but he was loved as not many have been loved, and though the stuff of the tabernacle was wearing thin he remained splendidly handsome, erect, dignified and courteous. He had lived a long life, and by the end he stood as one on the keystone of a bridge and held communication now with those who had crossed the flood, and now with those who were still crossing. He had his company both on this side of the river and on that. Whatever occasional glooms might fall upon him, the ascending stair was always at his feet. His was not an easy life, and could not, with his temperament, have been so. He had his hours in that valley of the shadow of death where faith seems to grow weary and sleep, when all things that are of the night wake up and speak. But the prevailing temper of his mind was eminently happy and hopeful, and few can have more perfectly fulfilled and realised the dreams and ambitions of their youth.

It is very difficult to write on this subject; but for the friendship with which he honoured me, and for the love I bore him, I must make the attempt. He was for many years one of the most constant and one of the most highly valued contributors to this journal.

I

Dr. Whyte's early life was a period of victorious struggle. He was born in the Thrums which Sir James Barrie has made immortal. He had little schooling, and worked as he could. He entered an atmosphere bleak from the outsider's point of view, but in reality full of eager intellectual and spiritual life. Next to his great and noble mother, his best friend was the Free Church minister of Airlie, the adjoining parish. The Rev. David White took the lad in hand, and provided for him some poorly paid teaching, besides helping him in other ways. At what was then considered an advanced age, he entered the University of Aberdeen. In spite of scanty acquirements and chances, he proved an ardent student, and graduated in four years with honours in philosophy. The bracing influence of Aberdeen stimulated him mightily, and the companionship of his fellow-townsman, A. O. Barrie, afterwards the distinguished Inspector of Schools, greatly helped him. Among the professors he was specially influenced by Bain, Geddes, and perhaps above all by Martin, who introduced him to Butler's *Analogy* and the study of the Epistle to the Romans.

Whyte had made up his mind on all essential points before he went to Aberdeen. He was a profoundly convinced Christian, and an ardent Free Churchman, and in these matters he remained of the same mind through all his long and loyal life. Loyal is, indeed, the word for him that comes most frequently to the mind. He never forsook a cause, never was deterred by any threat or loss from following the way of conviction, and never showed that he had any doubts or any fears. His favourite preacher in Aberdeen was the polished and cultivated Dr. A. D. Davidson. But he was not a little influenced by a young Baptist minister who had more power over the aspiring young men of the city than any other preacher. I refer to George S. Mee. Mr. Mee was the idol of James Macdonell and of many others not of equal intellectual rank. He became a journalist, however, and so a great preacher was lost to the Church.

Whyte determined to take his theological career at the New College, Edinburgh, of which he was afterwards to become the head. He had been used to read in the *British and Foreign Evangelical Review* and in Hugh Miller's writing in the *Witness*, and he threw himself with ardour into the atmosphere and the studies of the place. He maintained himself by acting as missionary assistant to Dr. Moody Stuart, of St. Luke's Free Church. He used to hear Candlish preach in the morning and Moody Stuart in the afternoon, and rightly thought himself fortunate. One of the most grateful of men, he particularly appreciated courtesy, and he was wont to say that Moody Stuart and others of his early friends treated him with the same punctilious respect when he was a poor unknown student as they did when he came to the front. The *Letters of Marcus Dods* give us some glimpses of Whyte as a divinity student. Whyte was always very frank, and he told Dods that he would never succeed as a preacher, urging him to establish a house for students where they might be trained, intellectually and otherwise. By that time Whyte had full hold of the Puritan theology. Dods characterised him as 'a fine, honest, doctrinal, outspoken, hearty fellow, that knows what he is himself, and does not require others to be much better, though he thinks they are.' Again: 'I like him for his honesty, his intelligence, his goodness and his real happiness of spirit. He has sorrows, but they don't cut very deep, as how could they in a fair-haired Scandinavian like him ?' Further, Dods notices: 'Whyte is a very high Calvinist and a lover of the Puritans, and would talk doctrine for a year on end.'

At that time in Edinburgh the publisher, James Nichol, was issuing a series of the works of the great Puritans. I believe that Whyte helped in the preparation of the index to Goodwin and in reading the proof-sheets. However this may be, there is no doubt that Goodwin was the master influence of his life. Whyte wrote himself in his later ministry the words:

> 'If I am to have some spare time to prepare myself finally before I die, I know the great masterpieces of salvation that I shall have set on the shelf nearest my bed. Shall I tell you some of them? My New Testament; my "Paradise"; my "Bunyan," and especially the Jordan scenes at the end; my *Saints' Rest,* and it is my old classfellow William Young's beautiful and fit edition; my life-long "Goodwin"; my "Rutherford"; my *Catechism on the Benefits of being a Believer;* my "Gerontius," and Olney and Wesley and kindred hymns. . . . Since I may any day die in a moment, let me have my hand on that heavenly shelf for a few minutes every day, and especially every night, lest the cock crow in my case suddenly.'

This desire was fulfilled. He was surrounded to the last with his cherished books, and 'Goodwin' was bound in morocco.

His power was fully recognised at once: he had a brief and brilliant ministry in Glasgow, but soon accepted a call from St. George's Free Church,

Edinburgh, to a colleagueship with Dr. Candlish. Candlish died in a very few years, and Whyte was left alone with the charge of the largest and most influential congregation of his Church.

III

Thus began one of the most memorable and wonderful ministries of which we have any record. I might well fill a volume with an account of his activities. He was a great centre of force, and his influence told all over his Church. By dint of genius and unremitting methodical labour he was able to attain the highest pulpit standard. He had strong health, a resolute will, and a consecrated mind and heart. Perhaps what struck the listener at first was his intense earnestness. There was fire in him, and it found its way. At his best his sermons were wonderful for their pure, true, genuine eloquence. They made a mighty impression. He had an absorbing belief in the power of the pulpit. He failed in no activity, but the pulpit was his throne. Sunday by Sunday he preached to great crowds from the fulness of his heart and mind. He also conducted what was called a prayer meeting, when he spoke for the most part extempore on vital subjects. He held great classes for young men and women, and showed the richness of his culture and the variety of his interests in a way which enthralled and attracted his hearers. He always refused, as far as he could, to take part in ecclesiastical business, but, of course, his influence told both directly and indirectly. He fascinated the young by the breadth of his intellectual sympathies, and speedily took his place at the head of the Edinburgh pulpit. One of his greatest services was the use he made of his influence over young ministers. He was alive and watchful to every sign of promise in young men. Though he could, and did, criticise severely, he preferred to encourage. But the burden of his counsel was always an exhortation to work, to work harder, to work incessantly, and to put the claims of the pulpit first. He rose early to do his own work. For years he wrote out all his sermons in full. He was convinced that ministers generally could accomplish far more than they did because their aim was not high enough.

IV

But on his ministry, generally, I must content myself with two remarks. It has to be borne in mind that at the background there was always that intensity of conviction and feeling which never fails to be contagious if it is matched with a character behind it.

As to the theme of his preaching, I have always thought that his own description was the best. He said a few years ago that he had received a message when walking in the Highlands that urged him to go on in his evangelical strain.

'What seemed to me to be a Divine Voice spoke with all-commanding power in my conscience, and said to me as clear as clear could be: "No! Go on, and flinch not! Go back and boldly finish the work that has been given you to do. Speak out and fear not. Make them, at any cost, to see themselves in God's holy law as in a glass. Do you that, for no one else will do it. No one else will so risk his life and his reputation as to do it. And you have not much of either left to risk. Go home and spend what is left of your life in your appointed task of showing My people their sin and their need of My Salvation." I shall never forget the exact spot where that clear command came to me, and where I got fresh authority and fresh encouragement to finish this part of my work. I know quite well that some of you think me little short of a monomaniac about sin. But I am not the first that has been so thought of and so spoken about. I am in good company, and I am content to be in it. Yes, you are quite right in that. For I most profoundly feel that I have been separated first to the personal experience of sin and then to the experimental preaching of sin above and beyond all my contemporaries in the pulpit of our day. And I think I know why that is so.'

That intense sense of sin never left him. In fact, if possible, it grew stronger and stronger.

To the same period belongs the following:—

'During a solitary walk along the hillside above the village of Durinish one day last September, all the way as I walked I was thinking about my own unceasing and ever-increasing temptations. Now as God would have it there had been a whole night of the densest sea-fog from the Atlantic, and the wet spray stood in millions of shining gems all over the spiders' webs that were woven all over the broom and the bracken, and the bushes of whin, and the bushes of heather. Had I not seen the scene with my own eyes I could not have believed it. The whole hillside was absolutely covered from top to bottom with spiders' webs past all counting up.'

He goes on to say that he thought of the blood-thirsty devil that lay watching for the silly flies at the hidden heart of every silvery web. The hillside that Sabbath afternoon was Satanic. 'So it is,' he said to himself, 'with thousands of Satan's death-spreading snares in the case of every human soul.'

I make a note on his theory of reading. He was a genuine bookman, if there was one in Scotland. The last words he wrote for publication were advice about reading. A bookman is one who has derived the intensest pleasure from books. But Whyte would have said that the true lover of books nourishes in his reading certain of the higher tendencies of his nature. He reads with a constant reference to his own views of life, and the confirmation, change and enlargement of his theories of life. He would have said that to read properly is to read with the highest aim of all—the expansion of reverence, obedience, and faith.

Whyte was not eager in encouraging young ministers to write. He thought that they should confine themselves to writing for the pulpit, and he himself steadily refused flattering offers from publishers, and wrote for his first book a commentary on the Shorter Catechism. I think he relaxed somewhat his strictness in these matters, and, in fact, he was an omnivorous reader himself.

Reading cannot be made the subject of laws and regulations, but strong in Whyte's mind was the motto, 'One thing I do.' The business of his life was to preach the gospel as he had received it, but in Scotland men like Stevenson and Barrie had no more eager friends and admirers than the great preacher of St. George's, and he could not help his own delight in fine things. I heard him read aloud some of the finest of Dante Rossetti's poems when they had just been published, and his magnificent library showed his catholicity. He was not narrow. His books show how far removed he was from narrowness. Every movement for liberty in his Church was supported by him, although he himself did not require any modification to his creed. At a considerable cost he supported Robertson Smith, and there were others. His culture was so wide and so true that it carried his words into places seldom reached by a Free Church minister. It was significant that he received, amidst universal congratulations, the freedom of the great city to which he gave his life. His own Church compelled him to accept their highest honour, the Principalship of the New College. It should never be forgotten in any sketch of his life that he had the most material aid from two colleagues, Dr. Hugh Black and Dr. John Kelman. Their association with Dr. Whyte was of the happiest kind, and he had no greater pleasure than in praising their work. So great was his influence in Edinburgh that hardly any one in the city was not touched by it directly or indirectly. Since Alexander Whyte preached his first sermon in St. George's from the words, 'Man goeth forth to his work and to his labour till the evening,' he faithfully pursued his appointed path, and he has been gently released at evenfall.

There is one word I should like to add. On thinking over our long association, it becomes clear to me that his main characteristic was his intense humility. He might seem austere, and he was austere at times. The burden of the world lay more heavily upon him than it lies on most, and before men he could at times denounce sin with terrible emphasis, but his face was often before God as a fountain of tears. He could not endure controversies with individuals. If he thought he had been carried away in some access of passion he humbled himself to the dust before the man whom he thought he had wronged. Evangelical humility is the note of all he preached and wrote. This was never a base humility. It never passed into a painful and haunting sense of inferiority. That feeling is the ruin of true humility, and Whyte, who was in all ways a just and faithful knight of God, had none of it. One thing for which he ardently prayed has been denied him. He longed with the whole passion of his powerful nature for a reunited Scottish Church. His death should lead to a greater visible earnestness in this vital matter. 'The King's business requireth haste.'

What a gift he was to his Church, to his nation! How wide were the irradiations of faith and love and hope and repentance that came from his intense and prayerful life! And he died as we should have wished him to die. Literally, he fell asleep in Jesus.

January 13, 1921.

INDEX

www.ingramcontent.com/pod-product-compliance
Lightning Source LLC
LaVergne TN
LVHW020530100826
845148LV00010B/1408
* 9 7 8 1 5 5 6 3 5 1 5 8 7 *